What Peop
WHEN A

M000308738

"*WHEN ADOPTION FAILS tells an uncommon tale of the not uncommon circumstance of child-selling in the white infant adoption market. While not all adoptees are so badly placed, those who were will find a welcome resonance in Farrisi's tale.*

"*Theresa relates her story in the passionate, colloquial and often humorous style of a native New Yorker. While the tone is decidedly bitter, it is not difficult to see through the pain and glean the message that adopted children, regardless of their provenance, should not be treated as commodities and that adopted adults likewise should not be treated as suspect, second-class citizens. Both adoption professionals and those in the adoption triad can benefit from the peculiar revelations of this frank, passionate journey.*"

—DAMSEL PLUM
Publications Chair, Bastard Nation

"*A poignant, personal story about the psychological costs of an adoption gone wrong.*"
—ROBERT PELC, Ph.D., A.B.P.P.

WHEN ADOPTION FAILS

pt 2017

To Dara

WHEN ADOPTION FAILS

I hope you enjoy reading
a bit of my life's story
with love
— Vida
xxxooo

THERESA RODRIGUEZ FARRISI

Homekeepers Publishing
Richland, Pennsylvania

Publishers' Cataloging in Publication

Farrisi, Theresa Rodriguez, 1962–
When adoption fails/Theresa Rodriguez Farrisi

ISBN 0-9656955-9-X pp. cm.
  1. Adoption. 2.Adopted children. 3. Adult adoptees 4. Adoptees-Identification. I. Title. II. Farrisi, Theresa Rodriguez. When Adoption Fails.
  Library of Congress Catalog Number 99-095442   362.734

WHEN ADOPTION FAILS
Theresa Rodriguez Farrisi

First Printing January 2001

Interior and exterior book design by Homekeepers Publishing, Richland, PA

ATTENTION ORGANIZATIONS, SOCIAL SERVICE PROFESSIONALS, AND ADOPTION SUPPORT GROUPS: Quantity discounts are available on bulk purchases of this book. Book excerpts can be created to meet your specific needs. For information please contact
Homekeepers Publishing, P.O. Box 439, Richland, PA 17087
877.285.4337 adoption@homekeepers.com
www.homekeepers.com

www. Dardsinger.com

To John Hudesman
Who understood

Table of Contents

The fallen vestige of her foliate time;
Browned leaves beneath; coarse needles of old pine
Once green and pungent; when her nests in spring
With peeping chicks, and swaying boughs, would sing.

So splendors fade, as does the daily light;
Of seed and growth and birth and bloom and height:
Such pastels surely rise to later blend
Into the morose darks of autumn end.

But when to earth her fullness drops like tears,
It thus becomes the soil of future years.

1984

Preface

I am writing this story so I can get it out and put it behind me. I have been told for years that I needed to write a book about my adoption experience and now is the time to do so. Actually, the more you can talk about your pain, the more healing you can receive and then the quicker you can go on to other places emotionally. If you keep it within, then it festers and you can never advance. I do so want to advance. I have finally laid it all out for the world to see and hear.

There are other parts of my life story which have nothing to do with my adoption (directly) and I have not gone into detail about those areas at all. Although the process of self-revelation is a little uncomfortable at times, I have felt that it is necessary to make my contribution to the literature on adoption and must do it this way.

I have meant to offend no one with my perspective and I pray my readers will be understanding and patient with our differing points of view should we be found to have any. I wish happiness and joy to all who adopt and for everyone who, with the best and noblest of intentions of the heart, desires to love and care for a child not born from their bodies. I wish you Godspeed and may He bring to your lives a child who needs you very much and whom you can love and cherish and provide for.

If you are a birth mother, I am proud of you and I thank you. You chose to give life, and chose to give that life to someone else, for reasons that are sometimes too painful to want to remember and too tragic to ever forget. This book is dedicated to every mother who chose life instead of abortion for their child and then made the choice to that let that child go.

If you are an adoptee, maybe you can see a little bit of yourself in my story, or maybe I have put into words things you have tried to say. I hope reading about my life will be cathartic and healing and empowering for you.

If you are adoptive parents, I hope this will help you understand the roots and wings of all adopted children. Do not hold against us the fact that we wish to dig or learn to fly.

Grace and peace be with you all.

INTRODUCTION
Sometimes I Feel Like
A Motherless Child

Adoption is a world of pretense and lies, bathed in lost hopes and crushed dreams, dreams which try to find their fulfillment through the bodies of the indigent or poor of this world and the progeny of their bodies. It seeks to make a fairy tale out of sad and lonely stories; perfect families out of other people's broken ones; and on occasion a happy home and secure future for a truly motherless and fatherless child. But not always.

While some on the receiving end of adoption may celebrate that an unfortunate woman became the conduit for a child that they now possess, the giving end will reveal an empty bed where a child might have slept; a dream for a happy life which must be fulfilled at the hands of others; a body and soul who endured creating and birthing and perhaps loving this product which is often all too quickly

1

transferred away to the upwardly mobile homes of Western affluence.

For those here and abroad who would rather kill a child untimely conceived, or of the unfavored sex, or too great a burden to raise, abortion or infanticide remain active alternatives. It is the birth mothers of adoptive children—brave women who by conviction or by love choose life, to bear a child in a difficult time or place—who are then the prized commodity, producing the needed offspring for the infertile, the big-hearted, or perhaps for those who simply waited far too long to try.

I have felt like a motherless child at times, but I always had two mothers, maybe even three. Bobbi bore me, suckled me, tried to care, then gave me away; Katharine got me and raised me and I grew to love her, although she ultimately also rejected me; between the two was Carmen, my foster mother, whose heart was broken when they gave me to her and then took me from her. And then there is me, the pawn in the chess game, the valuable blonde commodity, the "very desirable infant" who is the subject of this adoption story.

My story is of broken hearts and how they came to be broken through adoption.

CHAPTER ONE
All These Names

I could have been several people in my lifetime, and I indeed have been several people. At birth I was given one name; another upon adoption; another when I married, and finally, another when I changed my name in the 1990's. There was also room for at least one more change which in the course and turn of events never happened.

Once upon a time I was a little baby by the name of Vida Melissa Brown. Vida—because my mother kept looking through the baby books, came to the end before she found something that fit, and named me Vida, (it means life in Spanish, as well as the feminine of David in Hebrew); Melissa—who knows why, it means a bee; and Brown—because although my mother's ancestry was essentially Swiss-German, somebody on her father's side was Brown, an English name. So I started off as Vida, but did not for most of my present life end up as Vida, or Melissa, or Brown.

On the long form of any non-adopted person's birth certificate is a list of crucial and elemental information about one's self—date of birth, time of birth, place of birth, mother's name, her date of birth, occupation, father's name and info, doctor, and the all important birth certificate number—which will tell you what number birth you were in your particular locality for that particular year. An abstract of these records is kept (at least in New York City) in the Public Library and are public records. Normally a person goes through his entire life with that information unaltered—in fact, except for a name change, the other information on a person's birth certificate will not and cannot change. Except for adoptees.

When one is adopted, several things change on the birth certificate: the name given at birth (unless for some reason your adopted parents keep this), mother's and father's name, and certain identifying information. What generally stays the same: the location of birth, time of birth, doctor, and the birth certificate number. The worst of the abominations concerns the birth mother and the birth. No longer is the name of the woman who bore the child listed under "mother." It is erased and replaced with the name of the adoptive mother! Thus, according to this legal wizardry, the adoptive mother—who may have never been pregnant in her whole life—was in that hospital on the child's date of birth and is recorded as the one who gave birth! The original birth certificate is locked away and it becomes part of what is known in most states as "sealed" records. These are the records that adult adoptees all over the country have sought for years to unseal through protracted court battles and legislative action.

When I was eventually adopted, I joined the legions of illegitimate, bastard children, who are conferred a virtually new identity, replete with semblances of truth, hidden falsehoods, and outright lies, a make-believe neighborhood of instant happy families and grand illusions.

But on the way there, in my case, I had a temporary identity as the foster child of a family that almost adopted me. I could have ended up as Vida Howard, perhaps Vida Melissa Howard. This family had been willing to keep the name I was given at birth, but they were not ultimately allowed to adopt me.

As things went, I was adopted and my name became Theresa Emily Sedgwick Arluck, the name I had for over thirty years.

Finally, after much consternation, soul-searching, deliberation, heart-wrenching, and a legal petition, I became the person I am today, Vida Theresa Rodriguez Farrisi. Vida—because that name was mine before any other, and is my lawful, rightful name; Theresa—because I grew up as Theresa and for better or or worse I am Theresa; Rodriguez—because wherever my father is, he is a Rodriguez, and I am a Rodriguez, and can pass my heritage on to my children this way, or maybe even find him; and Farrisi—because my husband is half-Italian (I sure didn't marry him for his name!) Lest my readers think I use three names because I am a feminist, let me assure you that I do so for these reasons and not to prove any points!

So here I am. I often wonder why several fates or destinies introduced themselves to me only to disappear or turn the corner, why the odd and peculiar fate that befell me was chosen by the One who ultimately guides our destinies. My story is an attempt to reveal at least part of the machinations which destiny perhaps guided, or perhaps the shorter sight and shorter story for which destiny is a much larger part.

CHAPTER TWO
How I Was Adopted: Ed and Katharine

Once upon a time there was a couple who lived in New York City—a man and a woman who met during World War Two—he an Army psychologist and she an American Red Cross social worker assigned to deal with *"keeping the soldiers happy in the recreation room,"* as my Mama Mama, Katharine Sedgwick Auletta Rice Arluck, used to say. They both married late in life, Katharine being 10 years older than her husband Ed. It was a strange mixed marriage—Ed being a Jew, Katharine being a very Episcopalian, White Anglo-Saxon Protestant—and proud of it; Ed believing in everything spiritual but nothing "sacred," Katharine a good agnostic who left whatever Christianity she ever had behind with the "enlightenment" which often follows advanced education. Ed was a Jew of Russian descent whose family had come from Kiev; but due to anti-Semitism (and his following various writers including the racist Madame Blavatsky, who believed Jews to be inferior), he spurned his Judaism in favor of what he saw as "Christianity." This bizarre amalgamation of beliefs turned out to be the result of association with a religious cult called the Source Teaching Society— sort of what the New Age was before anybody had called it the New Age. He also spurned his Judaism because way back when, for some reason, his parents chose to *Bar Mitzvah* his older brother but when it came to be his turn, he never got *Bar Mitzvah*-ed. This evidently led to a great deal of bitterness in his heart toward his native religion and culture. In his teen years, so he told me, he "discovered" Jesus— this as a result of a sister who, in turn, has left Judaism in favor of this Source Teaching Society cult. Ed became deeply entrenched in this cult from his teen years up until the time I was brought into the Arluck home. Katharine fell in love with Ed somehow and married him, not because of his adhesion to this cult, but rather in spite of it. Katharine was well into her forties by the time they married and Ed was ten years younger. They were devotees of noted psychologist Carl Jung and actually went to Switzerland in the early '60's to study under his direct tutelage.

Edward Wiltcher Arluck was educated at CUNY—The City University of New York (when New York's own university was free, and really was the "poor man's Harvard"), and went on to receive both his Master's and Doctorate from Columbia. Like many Jewish intellectuals he had a bent for the Occult. He eventually taught psychology at Baruch College and had lots of private patients who came to our home. Katharine was educated at Tulane and Syracuse and became a high-ranking social worker in New York City, running half or most of Bellevue Hospital at one time and then eventually settling down to work at a certain adoption agency, the Children's Aid Society on East 22nd Street in Manhattan, through which I was eventually adopted.

In Katharine's pedigree were the likes of Pocahontas and John Rolfe and even Miles Standish (if that were possible!). Her family names were full of Britain—Royce, Sedgwick, Thompson. She mentioned the names of her family members—Charlotte, Elizabeth, Philomelia. I was supposed to be one of them, hence I was given not one but two middle names upon being adopted—Emily Sedgwick—which I often thought about using as a pseudonym if I ever wrote bad mysteries or romances.

When I finally got to college at Sarah Lawrence in the 1980's, I met a fellow who was a Sedgwick—the first I ever met—but always referred to him as "a cousin of my adoptive mother." I knew he wasn't related to me.

As it happened, the female leader of the Source Teaching Society (Ms. Cult Leader, who believed she was the reincarnation of Queen Nefertiti, which wasn't so bad, considering my father thought he was the incarnation of one of Jesus' apostles) died; and in her stead rose the likes of the aforementioned Mr. Cult

Leader, who held Ed in his clutches and dragged Katharine along for the ride. Her demise preceded my entrance into the Arluck household by some years. During this time Katharine and Ed were admonished that it would be good for their "spiritual growth" to have children. (I wish she had said it would have been good for their spiritual growth for them to have a couple of extra dogs or cats!)

Since they were too old to bear children themselves (and along the way they did lose a child in a late pregnancy, whom they named Edward Junior), adoption was the only logical conclusion. Even more so since Katharine worked at an adoption agency. It never occurred to me until just now, but I wonder if she didn't get a job there with the intention of getting them to let her have a baby or two, even though she was well past the cut-off age for prospective adoptive parents. Since Katharine was born in 1908, she was 54 when I was born, 55 by the time I was actually taken into their household, and 57 by the time they got around to getting my adopted brother Billy.

Ed was a cousin—I think even a first cousin but could have been a second cousin—of Hyman Arluck, son of a Synagogue cantor from Buffalo, New York, who became better known in the music industry during the '30's and '40's as Harold Arlen. We owe *Stormy Weather, Paper Moon, Somewhere Over The Rainbow* and the whole *Wizard of OZ* score to this cousin of my father Ed.

Katharine really was from another age. She always told me how in her childhood the milkman came to her house with milk (and I do also remember milkmen in our upstate country house even into the 1960's) and the cream being so thick at the top that it would push the little paper cap off the top of the very cold glass bottles. She also always reminded me that they didn't have penicillin or antibiotics in her childhood and she nearly lost her arm because of a bad childhood fall she sustained in an old barn. Her right arm was subsequently deformed at the elbow and it hung, unable to be extended, at a forty-five-degree angle for the rest of her life.

You could also count on her to use peculiar expressions from by-gone days, such as *"everything is copacetic,"* or *"he should have his head examined,"* or *"the whole kit and kaboodle,"* or a discussion about *"mental defectives."*

One of her childhood pictures showed a little girl not unlike Anastasia Romanov or one of the other daughters of Czar Nicholas, in regal white lace, looking with large, unsmiling eyes from sepia-toned shadows. When other children had lullabies sung to them—*"Rock a Bye Baby"* and *"Bye baby Bunting"* perhaps, I had heard such songs as *"When the Red, Red Robin Goes Bob, Bob, Bobbin' Along"* and *"A Tisket, A Tasket"* and *"Qué Será, Será."* Her generation was to see the most tangible evidences of technological change in the history of the world. I grew up with constant reminders of an age that was very dead and was never going to return, and yet I grew to often yearn for it. I was often sheltered and quite naive about the world around me, and although I developed a love for the fine arts, I lacked any involvement in, and little knowledge of, modern popular culture (which was probably just as well!).

Ed could never really get away from being Jewish, although he tried pretty hard. I think he was one of those people who actually took a class to try to get rid of their Brooklyn Jewish accent. We were never supposed to tell anyone he was really Jewish, or where his ancestors were really from, so they made up this story about his family being from "Alsace-Lorraine," the frontier region between France, Germany, Belgium and Switzerland. At the same time Katharine always went over the story of how Ed's Jewish mother Tessie beat a Russian Cossack soldier over the head with a mortar and pestle during one of the many anti-Jewish pogroms of the late 1800's and early 1900's.

So the Russian Jew from Kiev, who grew up like so many American Jews—in Brooklyn—becomes some kind of Everyman, a kind of pan-European, living off of Gramercy Park in New York. We sure did, however, eat a lot of bagels and lox, latkes with applesauce and sour cream, borscht and matzoah growing up.

My father wore wigs as did my mother. I suppose he went bald relatively early in life, so he got a series of toupees to wear in order to give the appearance of not being as old as he really was. This started when I was in grade school. He had three of them, I think, and didn't he give them all names?

So having parents who were trying to fake being younger than they really were, in order to fake being my parents, which they never were, with a lineage and ancestry that were being faked, along with an identity that was being faked, one can easily suppose why I could want to find out the real story—who I really was, why I really was who I was, why I wasn't who I was being made to be.

CHAPTER THREE
What Is And Never Should Have Been

I had grown up knowing I was very much adopted. It was kind of obvious anyway because my adopted parents were over fifty years older than I was. And it was obvious to everyone around me also, so I was the object of a lot of questioning growing up. *"Oh, are those your grand-parents?"* " *Who is your real mother?"* And so on. Like any child in my situation I had an honest curiosity about these things and wondered often who my "real" mother was. Katharine wove mysterious, tantalizing yarns about a pretty, blonde-haired, blue-eyed sixteen-year old girl who wasn't able to keep me. I also heard about tests I was given to make sure I "had no Negro blood" (which I always wondered about), and about a grandmother who wanted me but wasn't allowed to adopt me. Then I heard further tales of a foster family who had older boys but no girls—a nurse, who wanted me very much—who gave me too much iron and made all my baby teeth black—of my adoptive parents' involvement in a strange religious "community" run by a guy who, based on what I now understand about cults, would be great competition for David Koresh, impregnating women in his group and fathering all these kids and sucking people under. Katharine always told me that the last time she spoke to Mr. Cult Leader was the day they brought me home from the adoption agency and he called for some reason and she said "f——off!" (I think she prided herself for this display of good old Yiddish *chutzpah*—unprecedented nerve—as this type of demeanor was something completely out of character for my well-bred, Mayflower Society mama).

She was always worried that Mr. Cult would come around and try to get a hold of me. *"Don't you know I am your leader? that I am the Christ?"* he would say to her. Katharine considered it a sign of victory that she could curse at him and hang up the phone and then never talk to him again for another nearly thirty years. She used to rub it in all the time.

Often I would be at park playing, or in some other public venue and see some very pretty blonde lady and wonder *"Is she my mother?" "Could she be my mother?"* And I think I remember once coming home crying because I saw a lady who I was sure was my mother. Anyway, Katharine always said she would help me find my "real" mother someday if I wanted to find her—but that I should probably expect to find white trash at the end of my search and not anything of which to be especially proud. She often wondered why I should be interested in finding a kind of Dickensian equivalent in America or something—some ugly, dirty, sinister member of the Caucasian underworld.

During one of our rounds of verbal terror, which were routine in the Arluck household, I remember Katharine blurting out: *"You are nothing but common white trash. Brown. Melissa Brown. That's who you were, what your name was. Brown's as plain a name, blah blah blah....."* I covered my ears and begged her as I was crying not to go on with this. But I did manage to remember the Melissa Brown part and tucked that away for further future reference. (Katharine had evidently lost the "Vida" part of my original name within her aging memory.)

So what I had was this, growing up, according to Katharine: I was the illegitimate product of a blonde-haired, blue-eyed Midwestern girl of sixteen, who was of low social standing and unable to keep me. I was put up for adoption and stayed with a foster family, the mother of which was a nurse who was perhaps over-protective or liked to do too much to me and for me, and gave me too much iron, which ruined my teeth. My name was Melissa Brown. I was adopted when I was thirteen months old and had been in at least one foster home up until my adoption. That was pretty much about it. Oh, and Katharine did always manage to say how pretty my mother was.

From a philosophical standpoint, she would tell me that since she and Ed were not able to have children, I came to her by way of this other woman's body, and that I (my soul) was meant to be with them. Ed, on the other hand, often said that the worst thing they ever did was adopt me, and that if they knew what a little sh-t I would have turned out to be they would not have adopted me in the first place. And that I was not their daughter, but *"a live-in border."*

I suppose I always knew that I would search for my real mother someday. I was very, very curious to see this very pretty blonde lady. After all, Katharine was old and wore wigs and I did not look at all like her, and because she dyed her hair (or wore wigs that were) blonde she always said how we looked alike because we both had "ash-blonde" hair. I knew it was a scam and hated the pretense that I was her child, that I came from blue-blood, Daughters of the American Revolution, old mon-eyed, Royce (as in Rolls-Royce) stock, and so on. (Katharine's maiden name—Rice—is a variant of Royce.) I knew I was not those things, but as a child and youth I could not articulate my awareness of this or understand why I felt so very much unlike the family I grew up with. When Katharine would go on about her own very blue-blood heritage and expected me to take it on as my own, I knew I could not. Perhaps this is why I spurned boarding school at Margaret Hall in Kentucky and life as a would-be debutante and coming-out parties and the whole thing. She had that all planned for me, but by the time I was fifteen years old I was already moved out and supporting myself.

During the years that I was finishing high school, I did try to start searching for my "real mother." I had heard about The ALMA Society (the Adoptees Liberty Movement Association)—I think because Katharine herself was the one who told me about it. I applied for membership only to find I had to be eighteen—even if I was an emancipated minor, as I was at the time—before I could receive search assistance from them.

Because of this I let it go for many years, during which time I became a Christian, and began praying very hard that God Himself would allow me to find her, wherever she was. I did not actually, formally search until I was twenty-two, and the whole process once I got started lasted all of four months until I found her.

CHAPTER FOUR
Sitting Here In Limbo

"Child Adoption Service of the
New York State Charities Aid Association
Psychological Examination
March 18, 1963
Vida Brown

Chronological age:
8 months 2 days (35 weeks)

Vida is a very attractive infant with blonde hair, blue eyes, and pink complexion. She was responsive, smiled readily, vocalized and reached for objects which she carried to the mouth or banged on the table. She coughed a light cough several times during the session. According to the foster mother Vida eats and sleeps well and is fairly easy to take care of. She can say dada and name, creeps around the floor and pulls up in the playpen making a few steps holding on.

The results of the examination place Vida in the average to high average group.

Vida is a very attractive infant who shows average to high average development and is suitable for adoption at an early age. Her asthmatic condition presents a problem and the prospective parents will, of course, need to be apprised of the risks involved.

Medical Examination 3/18/63
Impression: good general condition. Questionable asthmatic condition. Child had 2 moderately severe episodes of asthmatic bronchitis with wheezing, at age of 2 and 3 months, both times responded with adrenaline injection. No severe episodes since then. No other serious illness. Mother asthmatic. Child with frequent upper respiratory infections."

(Bobbi gave me away between two and three months of age.)

There is a woman out there whom I have never met, who cared for me during the better part of my early infancy, who loved me and wanted me but was not allowed to raise me. Of all the figures in my story perhaps Carmen Howard is the most tragic, because of all players her heart was the most broken and hers dealt the hardest deal.

Carmen Berrios Howard, evidently of Hispanic descent, had two boys but was not able to have any more children and wanted a girl. I was placed with her family, possibly, in an effort to achieve perceived racial or ethnic equivalence to my own makeup, during the time that Bobbi was allowed to figure out if she really wanted to sign me away or not. This woman clearly loved me, and my heart aches for the sorrow she must have undergone in loosing me. I also wonder about the probably very happy life I might have had with her, and how life might have been as Vida Howard.

I have portions of the Department of Welfare transcript of my mother Bobbi's case history as follows (bear in mind that I had been Carmen Howard's foster child for over eleven months and I was over a year old by the time of this writing):

"*8/13/63 I received message that Vida Brown was to be transferred to a foster home with SCCA on 8/15/63.*

8/15/63 I went to the Howard household. Mrs. Howard was so upset about the baby's being taken from her that she didn't want to talk to the caseworker about it. She handed the baby to the caseworker and said goodbye.

Mrs. Howard advised that this caseworker left her no hopes for being able to adopt this baby. I agreed with this. Family advised they had contacted lawyers and assemblymen and would try to fight to get this baby. They felt the difference of religion should be overlooked since Vida had not been approved medically by the doctor at the Division of Home Finding, and that she had given Vida such good care and Vida needed her. Mrs. Howard advised that <u>her husband had called SCCA to speak about their chances to be interviewed but were rejected</u> (my emphasis).

Mrs. Howard spoke about contacting her mother (this means Bobbi) *privately. I strongly advised against this saying that for the protection of all this was not indicated. Mrs. Howard says she knows more about Vida and her situation than anyone thinks. She knows Vida is with SCCA because she went there for the psychological and medical testing. Once when mother came to see child, and worker was out of the room, mother began telling Mrs. Howard things that she thought mother shouldn't be talking about.*

Mrs. Howard stated she wanted to know when Vida was in an adoptive home. She thought at least she should have Vida until such a home is found so Vida doesn't have to move around so much.

I encouraged the Howards to remain foster parents and perhaps adopt a girl at an agency of their faith.

8/23/63 Caseworker wanted to know if mother [Bobbi] *had stated her religion and the religion she wanted child reared in. I looked at the surrender papers and <u>noted that a religious statement was not included.</u>* (My emphasis) *I checked in the case record and advised that mother had signed a statement of religious faith on 7/16/62 stating that she was an agnostic and that she wanted Vida raised in the Protestant faith.*

Caseworker advised that Vida has moved into an adoptive home during this past week.

Vida Melissa Brown, Polyclinic Hospital, White, Protestant, committed to Division of Home Finding for TC, and transferred to SCCA on 8/15/63 for adoptive planning, to be transferred to Indirect Adoption."

CHAPTER FIVE
Growing Up Adopted

I have always felt that I was on the outside of a clear-paned glass, looking in at activities within a functioning world but not being able to get in or to participate. Yet to the viewer at casual glance it must have seemed as if I really could, since they didn't see the invisible barrier separating us. I wasn't one of those children who was quickly and briskly adopted from birth, from a mother who perhaps never even got to touch, let alone hold, smell, kiss, or nurse her baby—no; my mother Bobbi wasn't just a conduit for the fulfilling of dreams that belonged to a richer, more affluent couple. She had been my mother, young as she was; mustering all of her nearly-seventeen years to try, and to want me, and to keep me. I had been with her for about two months before she gave me up; and when she did, I began what was a history of asthmatic attacks and lung conditions which abated only when I was finally adopted into the Arluck home. I do think I mourned what I perceived to be her death as a little baby. I remember being cold. Inside of me are those cries of panic and fear, and they have never left me. Even today as I near middle age, I can almost remember some remote sensations of being alone, in the cold, crying, every time I get into a hot bathtub. Somehow the heat of the tub, when I first get in, makes me get this rush of cold. I feel cold, like death. Primordially cold, like the beginning and end of time all wrapped up. The dawn of my memory and perhaps my psyche begins and ends in the shivering I experience in the water. The old tape plays, way, way back in the recesses of my memory. *Life-and-death-and-death-and-life*, I always say.

I was the with the Howard family until I was thirteen months old, and taken from them abruptly, so in a sense I lost two mothers before I was barely a year old. By the time I came to the Arlucks I was a little blonde-haired, blue-eyed baby, "very desirable" as the agency notes said. But if the first year of life makes you who you are, as many psychologists assert, then who I am was a series of rugs being pulled out from underneath me, or having security taken from me, or grabbing with my fists into the dry, open air.

I have no pictures of myself until I was three years old, which meant for the first two years the Arlucks had me they never once bothered to photograph me. The pictures I do have were necessary ones they had done for passport photos near my third birthday, in order for us all to take a luxury cruise to Europe just before they got my adopted brother that fall. Years later, when I found Bobbi, she gave me one of two pictures she had taken of me during those first two months, before I was given away.

None of this surprises me in retrospect. In fact, the majority of photos where the four of us "family members" were present show Ed in various states of disaffection towards me—standing behind me, holding my shoulder with one finger, pictures of him hugging my adopted brother while I am standing by, and so on. The greatest display of affection he showed me, I think, was how hard he would squeeze my hand as we would cross a busy New York intersection.

Well, he was old, and not an athletic type at all— I remember not a single outdoor game like tag or football or anything with him, ever. They paid for me to have lessons in those things—swimming, dance, tennis and of course, piano, for my budding musicianship. But we never played around or goofed or hugged that I can ever remember.

Ed once told me that the reason he could not love me, was that the day they came to adopt me, he reached out to me to pick me up. I resisted. I don't know too many year-old babies who, having been removed from the only home they knew just a few days before, would probably *like* being touched by a strange man—but since I recoiled at his first encounter with me, he decided, according to his own testimony, that he was not going to love me after that. At the same time I was told over the years that "karma" (or whatever they called it, "destiny" or "fate") intended me to be their child, because their bodies were unable to produce a child and my soul needed a body in which to reach them. I was also reminded how much I was not part of this crudely and unnaturally constructed family. Ed, as I mentioned before, used to tell me how I was *"not his daughter, but a live-in border,"* and that the *"worst mistake"* they ever made was in adopting me, and that if they *"had known what a little sh-t I was going to turn out to be, they would have never adopted"* me in the first place, and also that I had *"no capacity to love."* Throughout my childhood I was told many things like this and the tape still sometimes plays today.

As the years went on I was the subject of much of my adoptive father's rage, violent outburst of anger, authoritarian domination, and physical abuse. It was a convenient set-up for him, because he had a little girl who wanted very much to please her father, and believed everything he said as if God Himself had said it. I tried to figure out what I was doing wrong and how I could be a better little girl—the best little girl I could be. He was also a psychologist, which was the single strongest weapon used against my tender, forming mind. I would say, *"Daddy, since you use hypnosis in your counseling sessions, why don't you hypnotize me and make me the kind of daughter you want me to be?"*

As I got older, I asked him if he didn't have any emotional problems of his own; but he confidently replied that as a psychologist, he had to go through psychotherapy himself, and since he had been through psychotherapy already, he had dealt with all his problems and therefore didn't have any more problems. I was too young to logically refute these claims but at the time I did believe that he was always right, and I tried to find out how I was wrong and the cause of all the problems that happened in my childhood home. I did not see at all that I was dealing with an arrogant, unforgiving, conceited man, only that he was so smart, and knew so many things, that he had to be right.

Ed frequently compared me to my adoptive brother, which made for easy comparison I suppose. I was blonde; he was dark. I was gifted and intelligent; he was "learning disabled." My mother had cared for me and then gave me away; he was found, abandoned, in a Brooklyn garbage can. He displayed complete love and trust and outward affection to my adoptive parents; I remained on the outside looking in. He was also adopted within a few weeks of being born while I came to them well over a year old.

Katharine, ever the pragmatic one in her own bizarre way, always used to tell me that since Billy and I were not related by blood, when we grew up we could get married—*and then I wouldn't even have to change my last name!* As it turned out, I have nothing to do with the boy that grew up in the same household with me, haven't for over twenty years; I consider him merely someone with whom I happened to have shared a common name for some part of my life. He was also a causative factor in the final breakdown of my relationship with Katharine in the year before her death. And I do have to wonder if I would have made different and perhaps better life choices had that particular tape (and others equally as unforgettable) not have played in the back of my mind when I made some really big and consequential decisions in later years.

My adoptive mother venerated Ed. She never spoke a word against him in all the years I knew her. I never heard them argue or disagree in all the years I knew them. The arguments with Billy were few. But with me, it was as if I had been designated to crash in and ruin their whole lives, and they never ceased to remind me that I did.

I did grow very, very attached to Katharine. I have so many good and happy memories of her. She used to sing to me before bed, old songs from the big band era and the gay nineties—like *"Bicycle Built For Two,"* or *"Bye, Bye Blackbird,"* or *"Edelweiss,"* the song which I sang to her both at my wedding reception and on her deathbed. I am sure that part of the reason why I became a singer had to do with the nightly ritual she had of "schnoodles" on the belly and singing me to bed.

She would also make me breakfast in bed on my birthday, always taking time to cut a rose from a bush growing on the roof garden of our

Gramercy Park brownstone, or from the backyard in our country house, depending on where we were that particular summer. I will always remember those deeply-red roses with thorns. It was Katharine who always told me that if I ever had a bad dream (which I had a lot of) I could always come downstairs to their bedroom and "spoon" with her. I did spoon often, as I was both wild with bad dreams and a need to be loved. I have to believe that somewhere, though her mind became addlepated as her years wore on, and her bitterness towards me increased exponentially, that she did somehow love me. It would be too much to know otherwise.

I do remember trying to "spoon" with Ed but being told I must not take naps with him anymore. I often have wondered if he did not molest me in my sleep, as my brother did when I got older. When Ed died I found a sex manual in his office where he gave "therapy" to people, so the thought has always crossed my mind. I did wake up a few times in my teen years to find my adoptive brother's hands where they did not belong, which shocked and horrified and humiliated me, and I threatened to pummel him into the next life if he ever did it to me again. I moved out shortly after that time period, which occurred during the last episode of abuse, in which my father beat me.

I remained sanguine and hopeful during childhood, always trying to achieve approval from Ed and Katharine. I remember about the age of ten trying to make them breakfast in bed one day—as Katharine always did for me on those special days—and so one morning with Billy's help I made something with instant coffee, toast, and eggs. I brought it to them on a tray. I remember solemn faces and quiet eating. Years later Ed was to tell me that what gifts I ever made for him or gave him were meaningless, and he gave the example of the breakfast which I made him on that occasion—it was *"stone cold and inedible,"* but he *"ate it anyway."*

We lived during the week in a four-story brownstone in the heart of Manhattan—a true "carriage house" which had been converted from a rooming house into a private single dwelling. I grew up just two blocks east of the east end of Gramercy Park—*"a little too east to get a key to the park itself,"* Katharine always said. At one time they did own lavish brownstones right on Gramercy Park. It is the last private park in the city, and it is the heart of one of the truly nice neighborhoods left in Manhattan.

I remember many times when they would go away for the day (this is when I was a teenager already) and instead of being able to get into the house as most latchkey kids are able to do today, I had to wait outside for hours sometimes because they weren't home and I did not have a key to the house. They didn't trust me with with a key, not one house key during the five teen years I lived there. They actually kept the whole house locked up from me, as the various floors and rooms had doors which could close off large areas from the common hallways on each floor. The ground floor was my father's professional office and small apartment which always smelled dank with mildew. It was locked from the outside and from an inside doorway on the first floor. The first floor, which consisted of a huge formal living room, dining room, and kitchen, and also housed the bulk of the family heirlooms and treasures, was locked. The second floor, which consisted of my parent's bedroom, bath, and my father's library, was locked. The third floor consisted of the regular kitchen, my room, Billy's room, our bathroom and the family room. The upstairs kitchen was locked when they took a nap or went away. The family room was locked during naps or when they went out for evenings at the opera. Billy had a lock on his room. Even the door to the roof garden and patio was locked most of the time.

The only room without a lock was, of course, my room. I remember fights when all three of them were coming at me, and I ran to my room, only I was not able to lock my door, so I had to lean against it with all my might, with the three of them pushing on the door to get in to hurt me or yell or blame me. Eventually I found I could lock myself in the closet, which I did sometimes when I felt sorry for myself or wanted sympathy. I also remember laying on my bed and banging my head back and forth at night, side to side, side to side.

They kept their treasures and lives locked from me. Katharine, being from distantly-aristocratic heritage, coats-of-arms and all, had antique treasures and beautiful objects from ancient times, which were displayed before me on shelves which I could not reach and were forbidden to touch. Old pewter ware, English china, solid silver pieces, in addition to beautiful Persian rugs, and Chinese vases. All of these things went to an estate buyer, and not to me, when she died.

But of course, it was Ed who always told me that they were never going to leave any of their possessions to me when they died, or any of their money—that the only thing by law they were required to give me was *"one dollar."* When he would get into one of these fits he'd take a dollar bill out of his pocket, hold it up in front of me, and wag it back and forth in front of my face, shouting *"one dollar! one dollar!"*

I knew what was going on in my home wasn't like what went on in the homes of other girls I knew. I got scolded and sometimes hit for bringing home friends unannounced (and eventually I brought no one home). We watched my father beat the dog for defecating on the rug. I remember the Board of Health coming at one point because of reports of unsanitary conditions in the home. I remember being late from a play period at school and I was called into the principal's office—terrified at what my punishment at home would be. I cried hysterically, saying that my parents might *"take away my allowance or something."* I remember when I got hit by a car just a block from my home at the age of ten, that I lay on top of the car (where the driver stupidly put me), crying to my mother, and hoping they weren't going to be angry at me, *"I'm sorry ! I'm sorry! I'm sorry!!!!"*

CHAPTER SIX
Uncle John

Katharine was working at the adoption agency (presumably as a case worker) at the time I was adopted. Evidently she was able to pull some strings to get me and then my adoptive brother, because she was way past the normal age for adopting a child. In 1963 when Katharine took me into their home, I was a year old and she was fifty-five years old. When she got to adopting Billy she was fifty-seven years old. My father was something like 8 or 10 years younger than she was but even then he was well into his 40's with a new baby, plus he balded very early and looked much older than he really was—gray too, before he was 50. I have questioned all my life why this agency did not have the foresight to think that maybe this couple was too old to be taking a child into their lives at that time. Did they ask them why they wanted to adopt suddenly as they (or at least she) was approaching senior citizen status? Did they find out it was because of this cult they were involved in, that this female cult leader advised them to do it? Did the agency consider their motives or their capability to adequately raise two small children as they were getting old and gray and slow? Didn't they think it would look pretty obvious as we got older that they were not our biological parents—or worse yet, that they might not live to see their children to fruition or adulthood?

And so, we did have a what we called our "legal guardian" growing up—a protégé of Ed's (another promising young Jewish psychologist) whom Ed took under his wing. Apparently they were very close, as this man was more of the age to be a son to Ed than my adoptive brother could have ever been. Here we were, little kids and then there was our guardian (who I guess as we were growing up was in his early thirties), then there was Ed and Katharine—she in her sixties and he not far behind. Our guardian used to come and visit frequently, as I guess he was legally signed on to take care of us in the event that they died before we reached the age of eighteen. I knew about this arrangement for as far back as I can remember, and have always had fond memories of our guardian. He was a good, kind man who we called "Uncle John." He always used to throw me up in the air (something Ed was too old to do) and take us to Central Park and other places and make us feel welcome.

When I saw him in later years he told me that he stopped having anything to do with us (and I do remember this happening about the age of twelve or so) because of how Ed had treated me. It also helped me realize that I wasn't alone somehow. Being emotionally close to Ed, I am sure any kind of disagreement with him was difficult. Ed never was able to accept criticism in general, or admit that he had treated me badly, but always blamed the household state of affairs on me, on my emotional problems, my behavioral problems at school, my bad relationship with my adoptive brother, my bad relationship to him and to Katharine, or something other than his own contribution to the family dynamic.

But Uncle John was a happy light, a parting of the clouds during a childhood dark and often cold. I will always be grateful that he was there because perhaps I would have been much worse off if his kindness and caring hadn't been in my life during those formative years.

CHAPTER SEVEN
Protestant, Catholic or Cultic??

It seems that "religion" or matters spiritual have been an important factor in my life since I was a baby. I was denied adoption by my foster family because of religion: the agency never bothered to ask Bobbi if she would allow a Catholic family to adopt me (although years later she told me she would have said yes—this I still find incomprehensible!). And worst of all, the agency failed to delve a little more deeply into my adoptive parents' religious practices and beliefs. They might have discovered that they were Episcopalians in name only—that they were not Christian people, or "Protestant" (as they so legalistically insisted anyone adopting me had to be, based on Bobbi's initial statements) but that they were cultists, and Occultists, and New Agers (although the term hadn't come into usage yet). I have to hand it to Ed and Katharine that they were able to give the appearance of being all good things—church going, educated professionals of the highest caliber; financially secure.

The truth of the matter was that they were into Occult practices—séances, Ouija boards, white magic, reincarnation, Egyptology—all of which I was encouraged to take part in; we never prayed once to the Christian God of Heaven or read the Judeo-Christian Bible, though we consulted spirits "from the other side;" they had problems in terms of unforgiveness which made them incapable of dealing with any transgression on my part; they had money, but throughout my childhood—and even to the end of Katharine's life—their money was a kind of god to them, something that they prized and taunted me with and kept me from and denied me time and again, and finally, with my disinheritance, once and for all. What financial successes any child of affluent parents should be entitled to were denied me from childhood into and throughout my adulthood. They were probably unable to have children only because they got married so late and Katharine was pretty much past childbearing age before they really tried to have any. Their hearts were not into children; it was more of a decision of the head rather than of the heart. And when the heart-filled realities of dealing with an already broken child invaded their sterile plan for child rearing, they were not able to handle it.

Ed told me years later, he decided he could never love me, because I resisted his advances from the beginning, when I first came to them.

Suitable adoptive parents? You answer the question.

CHAPTER EIGHT
Emancipation Proclamation

Over the years Ed did a lot of things to me: I remember being hit with a big stick that had a nail sticking out of it (this was in our house in the country); of course he totally denied it and made me think I was crazy when I recollected the incident. Oh, some many times he made me wonder if I made all of this stuff up! He beat me once because I used a certain slang word, and he went on and on about it, shouting and yelling and whopping me good; one time he got angry at me and threw a box of tissues at me, and the point of the tissue box hit me right in the middle of my eyeball. My eyeball hurt so much that Katharine finally had to take me to the doctor. I lied, and told him that my brother had thrown the tissue box when it was Ed who did it. Katharine sat right there and lied along with me, chanting some little singsong about *"Iris-ilitis, Iris-ilitis, that's what you call it"*—inflammation of the Iris, like it was a badge of merit. As I got into adolescence I often called it something like "mind-rape." If I wasn't half as strong as I am I might have succumbed to the mental illness that was waiting in the wings for me.

In the early 70's the kids were wearing these things in New York called marshmallow shoes—big white-soled ugly things which you kept white with nurse's shoe polish. Like all the other kids I wanted to have marshmallow shoes. Finally I persuaded Ed to get me a pair, and he wasted no time getting me the cheapest and ugliest pair he could possible find— beige "pleather" shoes, 100% vinyl, but marshmallow shoes.

Maybe it's the way I walk—very toe-forward or what, but somehow after a short time of wearing these shoes a kind of slit developed where my big toe hit the front of the shoe. First it developed in my right shoe, then my left. I went to Ed to try to tell him (and naturally want to get another pair of shoes). I was told that I *"made the cuts on purpose"*—after I wanted these shoes so badly—and how could I be such a despicable child to deliberately cut shoes that he spent good money buying for me?

He cut two squares of clear contact paper and put them over the slits and I had to wear them, so embarrassingly, to school like that.

One day, when I was fifteen, I was in the kitchen (the groady, black-with-funk kitchen I grew up in), making some bacon. Oh, I fried the bacon in butter, which rubbed Ed the wrong way for some reason. Ed came in and had a fit about this, and a fight ensued where in the end he threw me into the bathroom. I fell on the metal towel rack, and he subsequently beat me with it, and I had two big welts on my right thigh. I decided that day, that I would report him for child abuse. I tried to leave the house but he stood in front of the door and he hid the towel rack in the closet near the front door. After some time and struggling he relented and I was able to go out the door—he shoved me out actually, with the towel rack in hand, out the door. I happened to have lived a block and a half from the police precinct, which was right down the street. I went in and reported him to the police and they told me that I could either be put into a group home or I would have to drop the charges. So I dropped the charges and moved out. And from that March of 1977 until my mother's death in 1985 I was not supported by them, they did not pay for college, they did not pay for my wedding, they did not provide any financial support for me, and I was finally cut off totally from every financial possibility or hope upon Katharine's death. This lack of support has affected my ability to become successful in the areas of my talents, abilities and passions, and has been a sad and sore spot in my heart for many years.

Ed said that he would never forgive me for going to the police about that incident, because I *"threatened to ruin his professional reputation"* as a psychologist and psychotherapist. He also said he had to stop teaching abnormal psychology because he was using me too much in his examples.

I did what I could do at fifteen, still a child, with the will of an Amazon. They had hurt me so much, and when I had no further reason to stay, I left. Initially they were willing to get me an apartment, which in my foolishness I refused. But after that, I only got a small Social Security stipend from the government for the next few years, and the rest of my support I earned by taking mother's helper, live-in au pair jobs, three of which I had before I finished high school, and several more during my college years.

CHAPTER NINE
Forgive Us As We Forgive Those

I did try to make peace with my adoptive parents over several periods before each of their deaths. After I became a Christian at age seventeen and my initial "asking them for forgiveness," our strained relationship continued until Ed's death in 1984 and ever more so until Katharine's death in 1995.

I was told by Ed that *he studied religion for fifty years, and now I was going to tell him about God?* and when I mentioned Jesus to him he said that *I had the audacity to tell him about Jesus? Because he was there!* (This because he was, as he used to explain, the reincarnation of one of Jesus' apostles. *Maybe Judas Escariot??*)

He died in 1984 and I cried and cried all the way home on the bus back from the memorial service. I felt I hadn't been a good enough daughter to him and that I had never pleased him. I probably never did and never could have. My grief is done now, and I have no further regrets as far as he was concerned.

I do regret that I caused Katharine any pain, because I am sure many adoptive mothers feel insecure about their role and abilities as a mother, for deep and understandable reasons—not being able to bear children, probably older, probably inexperienced; all these things make sense. In our case, she must have had a tremendous ambivalence about my desire to find my natural mother—on the one hand, she wanted to be unemotional and professional and allow me to satisfy my curiosities and longings; on the other hand, she was jealous of her, and resentful that I should have any desire to know this unknown person, a mere child, so beneath her in all the ways she felt were important. When I actually did find Bobbi and told Katharine about the experience, several months after Ed died, I don't think she ever forgave me for it, and if I could go back in time to the spring of 1985, I would have never told Katharine that I found Bobbi only that previous summer, nor would I have ever, ever told her in the years to come.

I went to many years of counseling over the hatred of the male and the masculine that formed within me, and did come around to a generalized forgiveness of the male sex and of my father Ed in particular. But to this day I avoid saying the words

"Dad" or "Daddy" (my children have a "Poppi"), and still can barely call God "Father," although "God" and "Lord" and "Jesus" spring easily from my lips.

CHAPTER TEN
La Vida Encuentra El Alma

When I was about nineteen I wanted to try again to find my natural mother. The first thing I did to begin searching in earnest was to get what records I could from the Children's Aid Society in New York, because at least Katharine worked there and it was the agency which handled the adoption. This information, which by law and in most instances is just about the only information which can be legally obtained from an adoption agency, is called the "non-identifying" information—which keeps identity a secret but offers the form and structure to one's adoption scenario. I received the following letter from the very kind social worker:

"April 12, 1982
Dear Miss Arluck:
I am writing in reply to your request for information about your background.

According to our records, you were born on July 16, 1962. At birth you weighed 5 lbs 10 oz, and you were 19 inches long.

Your mother was 16 years old when you were born. She was born in the Midwest and was Protestant. She had a difficult childhood. Her parents were divorced when she was 6 months old. She lived with her mother part of the time and with her maternal grandmother part of the time. At the age of 14, your mother left school. She worked as a waitress. She had suffered from bronchial asthma since childhood.

Your mother was 5'4" tall and had blonde hair and blue eyes. Her mother, your maternal grandmother, wanted to keep you. However, your mother felt that you would have a better home if you were adopted than if you stayed with her mother. She, herself, was in no position to keep you either financially or emotionally.

The information we have about your father came from your mother. She said he was 23 years old and was a Puerto Rican Catholic. He was a rock 'n roll songwriter, and had several of his songs recorded. He was 5'8" tall.

Your parents met each other in a restaurant. We know nothing of their relationship...

You remained with your mother from the time of your birth until September 28th, 1962 when you were two months old. At that time she took you to a public agency. The public agency placed you with a foster family. The foster family was very attached to you and wanted to keep you. However, the public agency made the decision to transfer you to State Charities Aid Association for adoptive planning (my emphasis). *On June 27th, 1963, when you were almost one year old, you were transferred to State Charities Aid Association. During your first year you had two asthmatic attacks, one at age two months and one at age 3 months. In addi-*

tion, you had a number of upper respiratory infections. On April 22, 1963 you had pneumonia.

The agency considered you to be a very desirable infant. You were described as a beautiful baby with big blue sparking eyes and soft blonde hair. One social worker described you as as "very pretty little girl who is bubbling over with good spirits and good health."(???? my question marks!!)

State Charities Aid placed you in a foster boarding home where you remained until August 22nd, 1963 when you were placed with the Arlucks. The Arlucks adopted you legally on December 30th, 1964.

I hope this information will be helpful to you. If I can be of further assistance, please contact me.

Sincerely, "

The letter was a revelation to me. For years I had wondered, since I was still somewhat fair-haired and blue-eyed but had olive skin if perhaps I wasn't Italian or Greek or some other Mediterranean ethnicity. And now I knew. Puerto Rico. Hispanic. Ha! *Me? The bogus blue-blood?*

And so I found out so many things that day: that I was born a very small baby, my mother was indeed sixteen, did indeed have blonde hair and blue eyes, did indeed come from the Midwest, that I had been in foster care, etc., etc. etc. It was a testament to the veracity of much of what Katharine had told me. And being both a singer and a writer, at least I finally knew where some of this endowment might have come from.

I immediately called the kind social worker to thank her and tell her how much this information had meant to me. I also tried to get even more information out of her, such as the state my mother was from and even perhaps her name, to no avail. I told her that I was going to search and find her, and I do believe she understood. Inasmuch as I have little respect for bureaucracy in general and social work pundits in particular, I did find this generous-hearted woman an encouragement to me in the long marathon ahead of me, cheering me on from the sidelines.

Finally I was twenty-two and I decided now was the time to find my mother. I had talked to Katharine about it beforehand, so she would know what my intentions were and so there would be no deceit on my part. Outwardly she applauded the idea and again offered any help she could. Inwardly, though she would never be honest enough to admit it, she seethed with jealousy, bitter envy, hatred, resentment, and unforgiveness towards me for doing it. I suppose my utter longing for this other mother of mine blinded me to Katharine's true feelings about my search. I do wish looking back she had been more honest with me about how this angered her, and that I had been wise enough to foresee the damage to our relationship which the issues regarding Bobbi could have caused and did cause.

It was the Spring of 1984 and the time was ripe for me to start the search. This thing had eaten away at me for too long by that point and I really needed to lay it to rest in my soul, to know who I was, and to find out why I was anyone at all. So I joined ALMA that spring and set off in February of that year to find out what I could at an ALMA meeting. The Adoptee's Liberty Movement of America was created by Florence Anna Fisher, an adoptee who through years of struggle found both natural parents and wanted to help others fulfill similar dreams.

It was a funny thing, that first ALMA meeting I attended. It was held in Midtown (midtown Manhattan, that is) in some kind of social club or Knights of Columbus building or something like that. It was near 5th Avenue (East, I think), but the location happened to be close to the 42nd Street Library—that beautiful, amazing edifice with the two Sphinx-like lions, Patience and Fortitude, waiting for you on either side of the entrance. What a gorgeous, amazing building, filled with such a glorious repository of knowledge.

After the meeting broke up I met for the first time with one of the ALMA people who said the very first thing I needed to do was find out my original name. (*What? How was I going to do that?*) The search assistant explained that since I happened to have been born in New York City, and Manhattan to be exact, I could actually go over to that incredible library and get this info, as certain records pertaining to births in New York City are kept there. *Man,* I thought. Since I brought my birth certificate with me (the one known as "Certification of Live Birth"), I was shown how the number on the certificate explains all about you—the year you were born, the county, and the number birth you were for that year in that county.

I knew I was birth number 24, 956 in the year 1962 in Manhattan, New York, by reading into the codes in the numbers on my birth certificate. So, even if you don't know anything about your original name, you could ostensibly start at birth certificate number 1 and work your way through every name in the birth records in the county you were born for the year you were born (which are not listed by number, but rather by last name), until you found your birth name. Fortunately in my case, I did have a hunch I was originally named "Brown," because of Katharine's rantings earlier in my life.

So I got to the library and found the reference room where the big books are kept, the nucleus from which an adoptee's information and identity springs. I went to the "Brown" listings and went through them with a paper ruler, looking for "24956". *Hmmmmm*, I thought. *Nothing*, I said, when I got to the end. *Let me check again, just to be sure.* So then I went through it again. Near the end of the Brown listing, I found my number: 24956. And the name was... Brown.....Vida. Vida! *Vida? What kind of a name is that?*, I asked myself.

So I kind of wobbled out of the door of the New York Public Library and toppled down the many steps in front, back to the ALMA meeting where everybody was reconvening after lunch. *Huh! I found my original name on my lunch break! Huh!* I told myself. As I started descending the library stairs, it finally dawned on me (probably a whole two minutes after I saw my name for the first time) that it was *La Vida*, as in "life" in Spanish (pronounced with a long *"eeeee"* sound) rather than Vida like Vidalia onions or something (which people even now often confuse and mispronounce like "Vyda", with a long *"iiiiiiiiii"* sound). *Hmmm, she named me "life" in Spanish, because my father was Puerto Rican.* That settled it. She had given my name meaning. She had tried to communicate something through that name.

The people at the ALMA meeting were pretty blown away that I had found my original name on the lunch break.

So, now what? I needed two things: the long form of my amended birth certificate, and the records from the hospital where I was born. Katharine had always said I was born in New York Hospital (why that one, I'll never know) but to know for sure, I had to get the long form of my birth certificate. The hospital, time of birth, birth date, and attending physician/midwife usually never changes when the original birth certificate is transformed into the falsified, bogus, adopted person's birth certificate.

I got the long form first, and was surprised to find out I was actually born at New York Polyclinic Hospital in the West 50's, which subsequently closed and had been converted into low-income housing units. I actually went there at one point and stood in front of the building (where you could see on the facade the old lettering that said "New York Polyclinic Hospital"—or the place where the old lettering was)—and I cried, and prayed, and said, *"I was in there once, and so was she. Oh God, will I ever see her again?"*

I found who "owned" the old records from New York Polyclinic, and wrote, asking for the birth records of "Vida Brown, dob 7/16/62," paid the twenty buck abstract fee and got my records. I think getting those records was even more amazing than getting my original name. Here were the real treasures: my mother's name, my grandmother's name (obscured, but traceable), the address where she lived when I was born, my father's "name" and "occupation" (which I almost immediately deduced were false), her date of birth, and place of birth. Wow, I really was born to her. I really was born there, to her, on July 16th, 1962. Yes, I really was somebody's flesh and blood child. And grandchild. She really was 16 years old. She really was from the Midwest. It all settled in and it felt very, very good to know even this much. Very, very good.

I did go on some wild goose chases—trying to locate both traces of my grandmother's name and the faked name of my father in old phone books—and even got a friend involved in looking through current Westchester County phone books (this was long before Internet phone directories!!). That stuff was definitely energy wasted, but I kept busy between requesting and receiving documents.

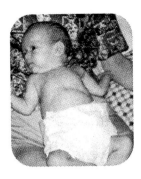

Vida at 2 months
September 1962
Just before
I was given away

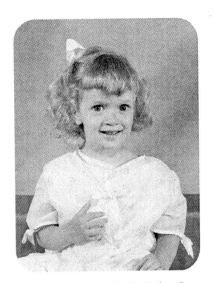

The "most desirable infant"
at 3, 1965

Sad Theresa,
age 5, 1967

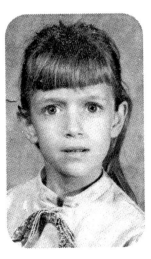

Sad Theresa,
age 7, 1969

Ed and Katharine,
circa 1950

Ed and Katharine, 1979

Dapper Ed, 1930's

Katharine, circa 1960

Ed and Katharine, 1979.
I think this is my favorite
picture of them both

"Mama Mama" 1994, age 86.
A year from the date of this
picture she was dead

4 yrs old, 1966.
Another triad, of which
I am on the outside

"Family" shot 1969. I am in the
back, away from the close,
main family triad

A typical paternal
"touch", 1970

A happier time, 1970.
Katharine is 62 and
I am 8

Uncle John, 1966

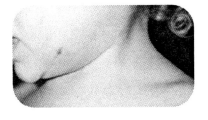

The dog bite that disinherited me,
1994

Bobbi, 1948, age 3

Bobbi, 1959, age 14

Me, 1998, age 36, on the left,
and Bobbi, 1976, age 31, on the right

Bobbi and me,
when we first met, 1984

1998

Nana (Bobbi's mom, my
grandmother)
3-4 years old

My grandmother (Nana)
and me, 1984

My sister Amanda,
1993

My brother Matt,
1989

My late great-grandmother,
Bernice (Nannie), circa 1950's

My sister Dana and me, 1984

The Farrisi family:
Tony, Theresa, and children (oldest to youngest):
Francesca Grace, Angelica Joy, Anthony Jr.,
Gloria Deo, Gabriella Rose and Sophia Theos
(born September 2000)

The next step was to get my mother's birth certificate, because that would tell us exactly where she was born, where she lived when she was born, her parents' names, etc. Because of the way she worded the information on my birth records, she was trying to make it seem that her maiden name was another name (actually my grandmother's married name) so originally I asked for a Roberta with this surname's certificate, only to be told no such person was born in Indiana at all within those dates mentioned. So I then wrote back for Roberta Brown's birth certificate, which I did finally get. The only thing I didn't like was that some of the search techniques involved and encouraged "little white lies" by saying you were your mother to get her records, and making up little stories as to why you didn't know what town you were born in. (This information was not in the birth records for some reason, and we had to have that.) I guess I was desperate to find her and complied with these things, but today I would not do this. I would find a completely honest way to get the info I wanted without having to tell or write an untruth. For what I did I pray God would forgive me even as I write this.

After I had my mother's birth certificate, I knew when, where, and to whom she was born, and the address she lived at at the time of her birth. Even though I still spent (wasted) time slaving over old phone books on microfiche in the big, beautiful Public Library (the same one that had my birth certificate info) the most concrete, direct information came from the birth certificates and hospital records. I had also gone to the address she had at the time I was born—and even found an older lady there who did remember a young girl and a baby many years ago, but nothing else; and even the second address given in the records—but that building became a condo and all records were destroyed. The first building was still basically an SRO (single-room occupancy hotel)-type place with no records going back over twenty years at that point. I had been in, and touched, three places I knew my mother had been with me, but still had no idea where she was or if I could ever find her.

I was then advised since we had one known address—the one in Indiana at the time of her birth in 1945—I was to get a "title search of the property" where my mother lived in Indiana. The logic is to trace owners of the property—if the house was sold to someone they might know where the other family moved to.

I was meeting a dear old friend for dinner. It was the 25th of June, 1984. I had been searching for approximately four months. I asked my friend if I could make a certain important call from her office before the day got any later. I called the office where those title search records are kept in that particular town and asked for the name of the person who lived at the address on my mother's birth certificate. She gave me the name of a certain Bernice M. K——— (I didn't notice it at that second, but this

Mrs. K——just happened to have the same first name—Bernice— as my mother's middle name).

So I called and the conversation went something like this:

"Hello, Mrs. Bernice K——?"

"Yes".

"Yes, hello, I am trying to find out some information about the person who owned the property you are living at in 1945. Do you know who owned the property you are living at in 1945?"

"Who?"

"The person who lived at the property you are now living at in 1945. Do you know anything about the people who used to live there?"

"Well, who is this?"

(I was told to make up a story about doing genealogical research and give a fake name. I never liked any of the fibbing/lying stuff, as I hate all lies, but here goes...)

"Uh, my name is... uh, Mary Brown, and I am trying to find a relative who lived at your address in 1945."

Silence.

"Well, nobody has lived in this house since 1945 but me. Who are you looking for?"

"Somebody by the name of Roberta Brown—"

"ROBERTA BROWN!!! That's my **granddaughter!!**"

In that moment, upon hearing those words, I knew that I had found her. I guess it took a minute to figure out I was actually talking to somebody I was related to, but she very quickly asked:

"Who did you say you were?"

(I tried to keep it a secret because I wasn't sure she'd let me know where her granddaughter was, so I kept up the stupid charade.)

"Uh, Mary Brown, a cousin of Roberta Brown..."

"Well, we don't have anybody in the family named Mary."

(Great. Now what.)

"Well, uh, do you know where Roberta is, so I can get a message to her?"

Somehow after all of that, she did tell me she was living in a certain town in Ohio and gave me the address. She said something about not wanting anyone to be hurt—as if she knew something—and I assured her I wanted to hurt no one. She knew I was somebody to her. I am sure that's why she gave me the information she did.

Bobbi had no phone at the time. I took my friend out to dinner in a near terror/joy/panic and then raced home on the train so fast, I never made it from Manhattan to the Bronx door to door that fast, ever, and probably nobody else ever did either. I then called Mrs. K——back. By that point I had figured out who Mrs. K——was—*my very own great-grandmother*, who by turn of fate had never moved from that house in the forty-odd years my mother had been alive. So my search, though I had wasted time on some non-concrete leads, was still pretty simple, in that I did not have to trace though forty-some years of name changes and addresses and God knows what else.

I told my great-grandmother that I was not Mary Brown, but that I was Theresa Arluck, her great-granddaughter, the child Roberta had given up for adoption, who was once named Vida. "*Yes, Vida. That's what she called you.*" Wow, what relief. It was really all together now. We talked more about my mother and a little about the family and I got an address where to write to her. I really wonder how I slept that night.

Finally I composed the following letter. I tried to make it a letter that would let her, and only her, know who I was, in the event some other person opened it who did not know she ever had a baby at sixteen that she gave up for adoption. Here is the essence of the letter:

"*6/26/84*

Dear Roberta:

We first met in New York in 1962 and I've wanted to get in touch with you for many years. Your grandmother Bernice gave me this address, and said you would be pleased to hear from me. Please call collect, etc., etc . . .

There is so much that I would like to share with you. You have been on my mind and in my heart for as long as I can remember, and still hold a place more dear within me than words can describe. I love you with all my heart. God bless you.

Love, Vida Melissa XXXOOO"

About four days later I got the phone call.

I really didn't know what to say!!! I don't remember at all what we said, except that I asked her what my ethnicity was and what my father's name was. She told me that my father's name was Miguel Antonio Rodriguez. Her ancestry lay among the Swiss-German Anabaptists on her mother's side and the mostly German on her father's side. What a combination, I was thinking. She then went into the story of my conception and her pregnancy with me, her birth, how she kept me for the first two months—and earnestly tried to make a go of it, of the difficult circumstances at the time, and her decision to let the Bureau of Child Welfare take me away. We went further into my grandmother, my siblings, her history up to that point, my history up to that point, and plans for me to come out to meet her.

I ended up going by train to see her, and we met again for the first time in twenty-two years. I knew it was her right away, and she knew it was me. I am glad we had a private meeting with no audience other than a few onlookers standing at the station platform. A rainbow appeared overhead as we drove to her house.

We hugged and touched a lot at first—reconnecting, sorting it all out. We went over every detail of both of our lives and the lives of my sisters and brother (all of whom she birthed and did not give away) and grandmother, with whom I am a very kindred spirit. We talked for days on end and I wonder if we ever slept that first week! We compared body parts, and had lots of laughs over stuff like that. It was so amazing that of her four children

I looked the most like her, even though I was the one not raised with her. We also compared temperament, favorite foods, colors, authors, childhoods, adolescences, loves and heartbreaks. I learned the whole saga of her side of the family and that very major part of part of why I am who I am.

Since then—over sixteen years now—we have seen each other as often as possible, written and talked by phone (and now email), do photos and whatever else we can do. I still feel insecure about our relationship and suppose I always will be. In some ways I feel I will always be a dispensable part of her life, and that our relationship, though very beautiful and precious to me, will never be a normal one. I have also come to observe that it is I who engenders and maintains the relationship, and that perhaps since I was once dispensable I shall always in some way be dispensable. If I did not make things happen, would they have ever happened, will they continue to happen?

Having met all of my maternal family (except for my paternal grandfather) I can say with certainty that I am one of my blood family, more than I could be of any other household or family. The puzzle is basically complete. I work now to fill in the missing pieces.

CHAPTER ELEVEN
Bobbi and Miguel

They met in a restaurant on the West Side of Manhattan in the Fall of 1961. My grandmother and my mother had moved to New York shortly before this and were settled in a single-room occupancy Hotel on West 79th Street. She was sixteen and working there as a waitress. He came in and ordered. She says he was a gorgeous looking guy, and she approached him saying. *"I think you look really neat and I would like to get to know you."* She has described him as almost foppish, Ricardo Montalban-looking, like he should have lace cuffs on his matador sleeves or something. He had black curly hair, brown eyes, and heralded from Puerto Rico, although his parents emigrated from *Castilla*, the Castille region of Spain. She recalls him mentioning the town of Santurce which is near San

Juan—he either lived there or was born there. She said his manners were impeccable. He wrote songs and told her he had some songs published. They got together. He was twenty-three years old.

They got together and somehow she became of his girls; when he was not writing songs he worked in the world's oldest profession and got her involved. My mother was beautiful, very well-developed, blonde-haired, green eyed, buxom and she became a prostitute and worked for him.

At then end of their tenure together—she says she can remember the night in question so it wasn't any of the other people from "service calls" or whatever—I was conceived.

Bobbi was and still a pristine example of what hippies were in the 60's—peace-loving, anti-establishment, engaging in certain cultural practices common to the '60's culture—although she spends her time actually being those things too much to try to be cool about it. She is acutely intelligent, a voracious reader, a bibliophile (with a collection of thousands of books), too down-to-earth to be over-ly intellectual but possessing a good and sharp mind, a lover of nature, a believer in astrology, reincarnation, more Eastern than Western religious thought, about as approachable and real and hon-est a person as you can possibly get. Pleasantly cyn-ical, openly homosexual, thrice divorced, incredi-bly sentimental, a mother of four children, the old-est of which is me.

What's so ironic about the whole thing is that Bobbi had forsaken her Christian heritage years before I re-entered her life (what little was left from ancestral traditional and upbringing) and then she gets this believer in Jesus who is the daughter she gave away. I connect to the mysticism and passion of Latin/Spanish faith, which might flow from my father's side, while at the same time I am sympathetic to the sentiments and doctrines of my mother's Swiss-German ancestors, who came to America in the 18th and 19th Centuries seeking religious asylum in Penn's Woods. Ultimately our ancestors moved away from Pennsylvania to settle in the Anabaptist enclaves of the Midwest.

I love the history of my mother's family, because I know that the blood of those dear Anabaptists flows through my veins. My Pennsylvania Dutch friends and neighbors are all cousins, I tell my kids. I tell the kids to wave at the Amish as they drive in their buggies past us, and say, *"Hello, cousins!"* Because we are.

According to the history compiled mainly by my grandmother, and genealogical records which I have compiled, we have direct ancestors on my mother's side who were Amish, Mennonite, and Dunkard Brethren—in fact, one of our ancestors was the founder and elder of one of the Dunkard Brethren churches in my mother's hometown. Our family names are Greib (Cripe), Martin, Miller, Ulrich, Mack. I have successfully traced the

Greib/Cripe family back ten generations to 1712 and the Mack family back seven generations to 1787.

Despite this interesting and unusual genealogy, my mother Bobbi had suffered a childhood full of loneliness, loss of dignity and self-esteem. Her adolescent years began in sorrow and in the middle of them I came along. Her living situation was not optimal at the time for raising a young child, but she told me years later that she really *did* want to keep me, that she *"could have gone to Cuba for an abortion"* if she hadn't wanted me, and although she did have a new boyfriend with whom she was spending a lot of time, she did keep me for two months before giving me away. I do not doubt any of these things. I only wonder why the social engineers didn't try to help her find better housing at the time, get her Medicaid, get her welfare, set her up in a manner that would have encouraged her to keep me rather than wrenching me away when I was still a newborn. My mother was not strong and I was obviously incapable of voicing my opinion other than through cries and tears. This positively boggles my mind to this day.

Miguel did offer to marry her and wanted to help my mother raise me. He even suggested that his sister in the Bronx could take me. My mother said no, because she did not love him, and because she was already onto other things by that point and her relationship with my father was simply not one of the deeper ones of her life. She never had a picture of him, never knew his birthday or exact year of birth, and I have nothing that connects me to him except a few vague memories my mother still possesses and a tiny gold bracelet he gave her to give to me. It is a gold baby bracelet with the name *"Vida"* engraved in script, with a little black onyx fist dangling from the side. The clenched fist is a Puerto Rican symbol of solidarity and good luck. Bobbi kept it all those years, and gave it to me when I found her. It is the only thing I have that connects me to my father besides his name. Someday I mean to put it in a shadow box and display it with some childhood pictures.

The only other connection, which may or may not be a connection, is the song *"If You Go Away"* which was attributed to Jaques Brel and recorded by Rod McKuen right around that same time period in 1961/1962. My mother told me that she remembers my father writing something on a piece of paper, handing it to her, and it was the words to *"If You Go Away."* How she ever figured out that Jacques Brel recorded it, I do not know. Maybe my father was a good con artist with an equally good memory for lyrics, or maybe he really did write it and sold the lyrics. I investigated this many times over the years to no avail—BMI, ASCAP, Paris, etc., etc.—to no avail.

I have tried many times over the years to find Miguel. It is a next to impossible task. I have no date of birth, no exact location of birth, no exact year of birth, no exact permutation of name he is using or has used (I mean, look at how many names I've had!), not to mention how common his name is, or how many ways Rodriguez can be spelled...with a *g*, a *q*, a *z*, or an *s*, or all or both or none????? It's kind of like trying to find the right John Smith, which is probably impossible without at least a birthdate.

I have come up with the following as the number of permutations I would have to search and have searched—*Miguel Antonio Rodriguez, Miguel Antonio Rodriquez, Miguel Antonio Rodrigues, Miguel Antonio Rodriques, Michael Rodriguez, Michael Rodriquez, Michael Rodiques, Michael Rodrigues...* *M. Rodriguez*, etc., etc., etc. Any search I do would probably have to be repeated seven times just to cover all bases, and even then I am grasping at straws, for wind blowing through my hands.

I have sat for many hours in front of old and new phone books, and now the Internet, with name after name of Miguel A. Rodriguez or some other variant in front of me, wondering if any of these guys could be my father. I have written email and letters to many and turned up nothing. My best guess is he is in prison, dead, or in Puerto Rico. Or maybe I have never gotten to him and he still would like to find me. Or maybe he has long ceased to wonder or care about little baby Vida who is now a mother of children herself.

Someday, I tell myself, if I am meant to find him, I will. If he is alive then I can still find him. If he is dead then his grave is somewhere, and I can find that. But he isn't getting any younger and neither am I. Maybe I would have been satisfied if she had only had at least a picture of him.

It's as good as being a test-tube baby, really.

CHAPTER TWELVE
Missing Mama Mama

Mama Mama has been dead, as of this writing, for over five years. She died when my third child, my only son, was a year old. Her death and what followed in the days immediately after her death were the hardest things I ever went through. For four years I could barely think about it, and if I ever talked about it, I cried and cried and there were no stopping the tears. But I noticed after four years that I could finally miss her, that in my dreams we are together, doing things, talking. I suppose the psychobabblists would say I am healing now, that my soul is trying to get to the acceptance phase of Elizabeth Kübler-Ross' five stages of death and dying. Well, maybe. I can see Mama Mama now. I can touch her in my dreams. But when I wake up the dread is very intense, because I know like a very good movie that you enjoy while you are watching it, the end does finally come and the credits roll. I struggle against all my religious beliefs; they seem to reject me and flee at these times. I wish I could unlock the mysteries of time travel—oh, if only I could go back to so many different points of my relationship with Katharine, how I might have done things differently, so that the final, horrible end would not be the bad dream I wake up from, and wake up into, every single day. Who has confounded time and space, so that I can go to this Oracle from the Lost Continent of Atlantis, and climb into a vessel which could take me back 5, maybe 10, maybe 15 years, or even more? I dream of such things but then the deadening thud is my waking every day.

I really loved my Mama Mama. She was the one who sang to me before bed, who let me climb into her bed after a bad dream, who sewed me delicate, silky and lacy clothes, who made me steak and hand-made French fries with plenty of salt. It was always a very weird, strained relationship, our two very disparate souls trying to get close to each other, always disappointing each other, always experiencing some bitter blow which would knock our progress back and kill our hopes for trying again. I loved her extraordinary intelligence; she reminds me in spirit so much of our present First Lady, Mrs. Clinton, a tough, bright, attractive woman with guts and strength and an assertiveness which defies most men today. That was Katharine, an early 20th-Century woman who bridged the gap to our growingly post-modern culture.

I loved talking to her—even if she really grew rambling and disoriented the more she aged. She was of the old school, of life before world wars and the speed with which relationships and experiences travel today. She could never understand why I needed to talk on the phone so much as a teenager, when, after all, *"in my day, a telephone never rang unless you were expecting someone to die. You only talk on the phone to plan a get-together, but you certainly don't* visit *on the phone!"* (Wonder what she'd think about the Internet!)

I sometimes wish she were still here so I could hear her talking to me. The older she got the more her gait deteriorated and I can see her in my mind now, almost dragging one leg behind the other. I can see her in the kitchen of her house, across the counter from me, where we would talk (or more accurately, she would talk and I would listen). She could tell me the same anecdote a hundred times and yet each time she was full of vibrant memory, articulate expression, and a fine sense of humor and wit. I really do miss talking with her and hearing her shuffling around.

But oh, I told my children as I cried and cried for weeks on end after she died, we do not have the past, but we have the future. I know. But the past can be a very unpleasant companion into the future. Sometimes it loves to taunt and to tease and sometimes it lends a pleasant distraction from the present; but by and large for me the past is a cruel and sadistic kind of leech, a kind of entity which derives its life from me, attaches itself to my soul but gives nothing back.

CHAPTER THIRTEEN
Show Me The Money

Did you ever have anybody dangle something in front of you—a candy bar, a special toy or something, when you were a kid, and then tell you that if you do this or that, you can have it? Well, what I had dangled in front of me was a little trinket called money. I think all my life I have waited for this money which never came, a wad of bills dangling in front of me—the stupid donkey—like a bunch of carrots. I can see the nice money in a wad and it sways back and forth as I pursue my dry and bumpy path but somehow no matter how hard I extend my neck I cannot reach it. It wags and it is wagged at me and was wagged at me for years and now I can never have it.

Katharine disinherited me of everything I was to have received from her just three months before she died. Do you want to know what it's like to live the end of a piece of great music—a concerto perhaps, the final cadences of something which makes you long and hope and pine, only to rest at the last fermata? At least with a CD you can play it again, but for me, I can play the sorry tape over in my mind and the sad final cadence does come, but there will never be a happy return to the major key in the recapitulation. There is no recapitulation for me, because she violated me, ruined my hope, robbed me, cheated me, and now here I am with such a smack on my soul's face, and such a reverse implosion in my heart! Like someone punched my guts from the inside out.

Katharine always dangled the money, much like Ed did when I was a kid. But when I was a kid it was an allowance, not the rightful passage of a near-fortune from parent to legal heir. When Ed died I also was disinherited (in his will of 1984) but since Katharine was still alive all the possessions and money went to her. It thus didn't matter much at the time, and I kind of had another chance as it were. She outlived him by eleven years although she was nine years older than he was. From 1984 until she died in 1995 she dangled that irresistible bauble in front of me—the jewel of economic security, which I hadn't had since I was a child; the jewel of being able to provide a stable dwelling place for my children; the jewel of being able to take care of some extensive medical procedures for myself which I have never been able to afford; the jewel of being in a position to help some needy people around the world and perhaps alleviate the suffering of some; the jewel of having, finally, my many and burdensome student loans paid for, and reap some of the benefits of having been adopted by these people, who were thus possessed of money but bereft in heart.

So I ended up in the end with no money and no heart either. I think Katharine's money was her heart, that's why she did not leave it to me when she died. Jesus did say that where your treasure is, that is where you will find your heart. Yes, her heart is now sitting in various accounts in a Florida bank, where I will never be able to use it for the good of anyone and where it will remain locked and closed to me without hope of ever, ever opening it.

You think I must be terribly wicked for a mother to disinherit me. I think all my childhood I did think that about myself. Even now I do question if I have some chronically wicked thing about me that would have caused her to cut me off and hurt me in such a way. But I did not ask to be adopted by this family; she chose to take me as her child; she should have let me have what was rightfully mine as her legal heir. What delight can someone take, who in leaving this material world and going where no possessions can accompany, denies her child the use of those things after he or she is gone? She would rather have thrown all her money in the toilet than give it to me I suppose.

I am amazed that loopholes in Florida law exist for senior citizens that allow rights of primogeniture—rights of the firstborn and all of that Medieval stuff—to be tossed to the wind, if a growingly feeble-minded octogenarian decides to play a game of spite or revenge with their worldly possessions and not pass them on. Are there no protections for adult children, simply if they are legal heirs? Apparently not, because it happened to me. Ah, it hurts to think that I had no rights whatsoever and my financial future was taken away from me with one signature—from one hard-hearted hand, stemming from an addlepated, confused, bitter woman about to die.

In my adult years my relationship with my adoptive mother was like that of a child sitting on the edge of a rail fence—either way you will fall off and hit the ground. I always tried to balance myself so I would not fall off. I always hoped I could keep hanging there in the middle before I fell off and the courses went against me again. But it didn't; I did not win the final game of odds.

Katharine demonstrated what would be known as "conditional" love (if you could really call "love" something which has to meet conditions). She would think about displaying favor to me if I stroked her the right way, sucked up to her, let her hear her own voice talking, not get in the way of any of her machinations. If I let her act as if she were a god or goddess this would greatly please her and I would (so I thought) be in her favor. It was during times when we got along that I was written into the will and the trust. I was supposed to get half of the sizable estate broken up into certain distributions until certain ages. Sometimes during the good periods of our relationship she would sit me down and explain my future to me: *"When I die, you will get this and such until you are thirty-five years old, then you get the whole kit and kaboodle* (as she used to say), *whatever is left, split between you and Billy."* In the back of my mind I knew how mercurial her feelings were towards me and how heavily her emotions or grudges or states of bitterness would play into any decision she would ever make, so I always took these pronouncements with a pretty big grain of salt. I knew from the bad times, when I had failed some part of whatever conditions she had laid out for me, that the pendulum could swing against me at any time or that I could surely fail her conditions for receiving the long-awaited material reward upon her death, and thus this so-called love.

CHAPTER FOURTEEN
Those Animals

There are people in the world who love animals more than they love people. They will sit and coddle a dog, let its saliva drip all over them, let the beast lick their faces and slime all over their mouths, who suffer through the stink that their bodies make on furniture or have to clean up accidents wherever they occur; these will picket animal hospitals which gently put overpopulated animals to sleep, or feel the pain of poor seals skinned alive by zealous hunters: but many of these same people would cringe at having to change a human baby's diaper, are repelled by the sight of a mother suckling her own child, quickly wipe the drool from a child's kiss off their faces, who barely bat an eyelash over the untold slaughter of living, unmedicated human babies who die in horrible pain by the thousands every day inside the bodies of their mothers through abortion; who care more for the rights of a whale or a spotted owl than that of a growing baby human. I think Katharine was one of these types of people for sure.

During all those years, when I was without health insurance or a way to treat some chronic medical conditions that I have had, Katharine's dogs never missed a veterinarian treatment or failed to have their bodily needs attended to. Oh! she would talk to the creatures with such meaning that I could see her almost tearing around the eyeballs as her heart would swell with waves of animal-loving passion. She would tell me how this or that dog or cat we had was the reincarnation of a previous creature or animal, or how these creatures would communicate with her in a special kind of animal language. It's no wonder that paganism is replete with the worship of all manner of beasts and spirits.

Katharine chose her dog over me and this is why I was disinherited. This woman—who took me to live in her home as a year-old child, who sang me to bed in childhood, who introduced me to a love of nature and the outdoors, who helped develop my intellect and aesthetic and cultural likes and dislikes, who both caused and dried so many of my tears, who taught me to speak and to think, and who was the dearest human soul in the world to me, chose at the end of her life, after a relationship spanning over thirty years, to cut me off from every material benefit she left in this world. She chose to leave me nothing, not a penny, not even Ed's "one dollar!" All of the early American pewter, the Rockingham China, the rare books, the antiques—all sold upon her death to an estate dealer; all the monies in estate tied up endlessly in mutual funds, waiting to be given— not to me, but only to my former brother's offspring (not even mine—as if they never existed!); all kind and happy memories of my life—where I could not help loving this peculiar, aged woman as my mother—pulverized under the tremendous boulder which she threw out of her heart and upon me the day she died.

A year before Katharine died the toll of age and atrophy of her being was beginning to really show. We were on good terms then; I was in the will fifty-fifty with Billy; I was getting the whole beautiful package of material things which I intended to use someday to own a home, get out of debt, get medical attention, provide for some of the less fortunate in the world, and make my family happy. Since it is no exaggeration that I had moved by that point 30 times or more since I was 15, the idea of settling down to a permanent dwelling for me and my growing family was something to really look forward to someday.

About ten years before that—also at a time when we were on good terms (i.e., I was in the will)—Katharine had an acute attack of congestive heart failure one afternoon, during the period when she lived in her upstate New York house, just before moving to Florida. She was breathing fluids from her lungs and then decided to lay on the couch, so she could look out the window at the herons flying over the backyard lake as she died. She really was going to die that day, but I did not want her to die that day, in front of me, as I stood there. Against her protestations I called an ambulance and she was saved to live another ten years and disinherit me at the end. So please, nobody say I was just in this for the money! When she was finally really dying, it was I who flew hundreds of miles to her bedside, while her son, who lived locally, was nowhere to be found. Katharine and I spent that last day together, as her body began its final breaths and functions, hacking up green gunk from inside her guts, as her eyes became utter pins and it seemed as if her soul had left long before her body gave out. I sang to her, as she had sung to me so many childhood nights; I rubbed her feet with lotion, as I had done so many times when I was a child—anointing her body for cremation I suppose; I lay down next to her on that skinny hospital bed and held that body which twenty-four hours into the future would exist no more. I talked into ears that I am not sure could hear, or perhaps could no longer respond. I encouraged her that peace with the Creator was still possible; that she could enter into His eternal life, even then; that there was room at the cross for her even yet, and that Jesus was waiting to forgive her.

As the early morning hours led to what the medical world calls Cheynne-Stokes breathing—that God-awful, bellow-y heaving of the lungs' final breath—the end was near. I knew my Mama Mama was going to be dead and I would never be able to talk to her again, or love her, or be with her, or listen to her talk, or take our many afternoon rides in the car looking at all the houses I longed to own, or try to gather love where I could from her, ever again. There was no other time, no other chances, it was all going to be over. The nurse and my mother's friend and caretaker took me out of the room at the very end and got me to a motel since they didn't want me to see the final moments. I remember how I could barely pull myself away from the threshold of that hospital room door as I wailed, *"Goodbye Mama! Goodbye Mama!"*—because she was really going to die, she was going to be dead in a few minutes and I wouldn't get to see my Mama Mama anymore. I just needed to say goodbye again, just one more time, then they pulled me away forever, and she died shortly thereafter while I napped at the motel.

Those funny studies they once did on monkeys remind me of how you can get attached to the weirdest things, how vulnerable humans are and how we share a kind of vulnerability for attachment with the higher functioning animals. It had something to do with a fake wire mama monkey and a forlorn living baby monkey. The baby hung and clung to this weird wire monkey because it was the only Mama it knew.

Mama Mama was my wire monkey, and I loved her so very, very much.

The next day, after a tortured sleep, I awoke to be informed by bank officer that I was *"disinherited, totally."* To this day I wonder if anything ever hit me as hard as that did. It was practically incomprehensible to me that it was really true. *Was there no hope of changing such a terrible pronouncement? How could it be? How could it be legal that she did that to me? Don't I have any rights as a legal daughter, albeit an adopted one?* My mind reeled with a thousand aching questions and a swirling whirlwind of total shock.

But it was not as if I had no inkling that it might happen, only that the banker lied to me during the year before she died (and she and I were in the final "off" period) and fooled me into thinking all was well with Katharine and the estate when it was not. (Three months before she died the bank entourage—Katharine used to call them "the pack"—had come to the hospital so they could help her sign away my inheritance.) It was already taken from me, and they knew it was coming, and led me to believe all was well until it was too late. I think I felt what some people must feel when they are sentenced after a criminal trial to life in jail without parole: there is simply no other fate. That's it. You can try to dream away the reality, try to go back in your mind to when the road forked and you could have gone the other way—and you do it a million times in your mind everyday after that—but no, there is nothing else, and you will wake up in that jail cell tomorrow, buddy, and the next tomorrow, and the next, and the next, until you die.

We get back to dogs now. I know any animal lovers among my readers will hate me for this, but if every creature on the face of the earth were suddenly irradiated and dropped off the planet, you would not see me bat an eyelash. I used to really love animals and was a vegetarian "love-animals-don't-eat-them" type in my teen years, but over time, partly due to severe animal allergies and asthma, and perhaps partly because of my experiences with people making gods out of their pets, I have grown to really detest creatures. Period. Sometimes I think it is when people cease to love their own offspring that they funnel their affection and devotion on beasts. So it was a dog that caused me to loose my inheritance.

The next-to-final incident revolved around the point at which we were called upon to help her come and live with us, because she was becoming more disoriented, unable to do for herself, and my adopted brother had been neglecting her and worse, details of which I will forgo. This was almost a year to the week before she died, and it was the last period of time I saw my mother walking, talking, existing as we know it.

She had some kind of a mutt dog—a large Golden Retriever-type dog, for which she would cook high-class tidbits, who pooped and peed everywhere, which she worshiped in her pantheon of creatures and spirits.

This particular dog one morning bit one of my daughters in the face. This was during the visit our whole family had made to Florida, just three weeks after the birth of my third child—at the behest of her dutiful and faithful friend and care-taker. Our purpose was to gather Katharine up and take her to Pennsylvania, get her house in Florida ready to be sold, and then have her live with us in a house she was to purchase and leave to us when she died.

Katherine coddled the diseased animal (who died six months later of a brain tumor) while my husband and I saw broken skin on my two-year old little girl's face. I mentioned something about "calling dog control," because my first thought was, if the dog was rabid my child could get sick or even die. Then the demons that drove Katharine (all her life, perhaps) rose up in syn-chrony and manifested themselves about her eye-balls. Believe me, demon-possessed people exist, and I saw one that morning. The rims of her eye-lids turned completely red in a circle, and she looked at me with the look of Legion; she told me square in the face, that if I called dog control that she *"would disinherit"* me and that I *"would never get anything"* from her ever again.

In that moment I think it all coalesced. Here was the woman who over thirty years before was handed a foster child, deep from within the quagmire of the child welfare system of New York City (a child who, moreover, was wrenched by that system from a perfectly good home and a foster mother who apparently really loved her), who now planned to disown that same child over the feelings for an aggressive, sick animal. All my life that God-forsaken money was dangled, that jewel, that trinket, that carrot—and I saw it dangling there too, in that moment.

NO! I said to myself. *NO! Does she think I am going to let her manipulate me now??? Cause me to choose her money over my child? NO! NO! NO! NO! Get thee and thy money behind me, Satan!*

And so I left the room and I called dog control. After we left her house and went back to Pennsylvania the dog was house-quarantined by local authorities, because the animal had bitten a child before it attacked our daughter. Six months later it was dead. Katharine never, ever worried about my daughter's bite wound (or my children at all, for that matter). It was as if my children never existed.

We left her in Florida and came home. During that final year I only spoke to her perhaps a half a dozen more times until the day before she had the last stroke—about a day before she died. Before this final point, we spent about nine months in silence with one another, as I was assured by the banker that she couldn't really disinherit me and not to worry about it. I wanted her to cool off so we could try to patch things up, which I thought we were doing, and then she was dead.

When she finally got around to disinheriting me, she had lost so much mental and physical capacity that I am really surprised the amended documents stood up in my later protracted court battle, which I ultimately lost. (Years later I ended up with a paltry "settlement" which was the bank's way of avoiding any further litigation.) I still am utterly amazed that one signature can destroy the relationship of a lifetime and the material benefits to which a legal heir should be entitled.

CHAPTER FIFTEEN
For Bureaucrats and Do-Gooders Who Need To Justify Their Existence

I wish that the social engineers who had handled my foster care period had been more sensitive to the growing bond between me and my foster mother, not ignored the fact that this woman wanted to adopt me, and had taken extra measures to have allowed what seemed like a perfectly natural adoption to take place. When I found Bobbi in 1984, she had assumed that my name had been kept Vida (something the foster family had agreed to do). It was a real shock to her to find out I had not only been adopted by an entirely different, non-Catholic couple, but that my name was changed to Theresa. She would have had no problem with the Howards adopting me—indeed, this was the family she thought had adopted me. This segment of the story remains a mystery to me.

There were a number of losers in the case of my adoption. The social service machine failed me, in placing me legally with a couple and a situation with an extraordinary potential for dysfunction; they denied me what I could see now as a "normal" upbringing with my foster family; they misled my birth mother into thinking it was this certain family who adopted me, and that her parting wishes we kept, when they were not; and I now bear the marks of childhood, and parental relationship, scarred by all things ugly, bitter and cruel, rather than by happiness and love.

The second losers were the foster family, who had me from the time I was two and a half months old until I was a year old. After I had my first child it began to dawn on me, as I watched her grow that first year, that neither Katharine nor Bobbi had me during that same time period; it was Carmen who saw me first sit up, crawl, take my first steps, say *dada*, cut my teeth, and had cared for me during that crucial and critical first year. And I was taken from this mother over a misunderstanding or perhaps insensitive legalism. I wonder how much my foster mother cried and what these heartless bureaucrats did to wound her. As with Miguel, I do put some effort every now and then into finding her, and have found a good deal of information already.

Being a foster parent is a risky thing I think. You naturally get attached to these kids that you are not generally allowed to adopt; they are wrenched from you at any time; you are supposed to keep your distance while providing a semblance of caring and happy home life—all of this as if you are a robot or emotional whore, paid to perform or not perform at will.

And then there's the foster kid, who becomes a yo-yo in machine of child "welfare"—often wrenched any number of times from home situation to home situation, all in the name of providing normalcy. Certainly having your roots torn apart many times in childhood cannot be good for any child. Makes me wonder sometimes if one orphanage is better than five foster homes. Certainly the factors of human emotion and attachment and even— Heaven forbid!—love—are ignored. Bureaucrats seem to be more interested in proving they are good little social workers playing a chess game with people's lives than considering the long-term consequences of their actions. Place this child here; move this child there; remove this child from this home; replace it with this child; take this child away; give this child to this mother; oh, maybe not, let's try someone else—leaving behind a trail of tears and broken hearts and shattered destinies.

Oh, what can be done so that a child forms an attachment to one set of parents or one mother alone, from as early an age as possible, and never, ever taken away?

CHAPTER SIXTEEN
Onward Christian Soldiers

We are supposed to fight our battles with love, not with weapons which can hurt one another. At this point I am trying to go on with love in my heart but I am not fully healed of my adoption experience and perhaps in this lifetime I never will be. The writing of this story has been good and I can look at the past more now and it doesn't scare me as much as it once did.

I wish that bureaucracies of all sizes would pay close heed to the delicate and vulnerable sensibilities that involve all people in foster care and adoption— how quickly and deeply people of all ages can become attached to one another and how damaging is the destruction of any bonds that so quickly and deeply form. Some people seeking to adopt may be doing so for reasons of power, emotional need, religious fervor, or cold philosophical conclusions. Perhaps there ought to be more careful background checks on prospective parents for signs of these truly self-centered motives. A child will attach quickly and deeply, because he needs to; the baby monkey and the wire mama. It is cruel both to create the wire mama and let the monkey get attached to it.

Even biological parents and children have clashes and conflict, but I suspect there is a great deal of incompatibility within many adoptive relationships. Some children simply lived too long with someone else—someone that they loved—before being adopted, and cannot love again; some never had a person to love very well or long enough; sometimes differing cultural or ethnic makeups can present future problems, as roots and wings expand within the adoptive person's psyche.

Adoption results from an imperfect situation, where the biological parents are not present or able, or perhaps convinced they are not able, to raise the children they conceive. I do firmly believe having both male and female biological parents to be truly the best and optimum scenario into which a child can be raised.

Adoption therefore is a kind of second best for everyone involved—for the mother who is perhaps unable to conceive, and thus wants to raise the child born from another woman's body; for the child who has to be torn from the womb and arms of the one who bare him or her; for the mother who conceived, spent nine months carrying, then bearing, and then giving away her progeny; for the fathers, who so much of the time simply abrogate any responsibility for the children they so carelessly produce, and for which society seems to place so little penalty.

I wonder sometimes about Vida Howard, a Catholic girl from the Bronx, the. girl I never became. No doubt I'd still be singing and writing, but it would not be this story. Perhaps it would have been one called *When Adoption Succeeds* and I'd be singing happier songs. If I ever find my foster mother I suppose I will know if this is true.

In a sense, I have died to both mothers, or they died to me. When Bobbie gave me away, it was as if she died, and our reunion in my adulthood has felt more like a phantom or dream than a living reality. When I lost Katharine she really did die. In some ways I feel like I have no mother at all, or two half-mothers, part-mothers, somewhat-mothers, both for whom I never was truly acceptable or bearable.

But if Bobbi and Miguel—together—had kept me—now that is something to ponder.

Acknowledgements:

Karl Zimmer of ALMA, who helped me find Bobbi in 1984.

Kathy Henry, who helped me during the search for Bobbi and for being a prayerful, supportive friend during those tumultuous '80s years.

Demetra Kritas Dunlop, who has encouraged me more than anybody ever could, in every way a person can ever be encouraged. *When the winds wafts our seeded shafts, we bend in synchrony.*

Carol Briggs, who cared for Katharine when I could not, helped ease the pain of death and rejection, stuck up for me when I needed justification and helped make the transition to life without her.

Eileen Pereira Arndt, who has known these longings of my heart before anyone else, and has shared my griefs and joys like no other. *Traveling further than the previous, and surviving a bitterer storm.*

Joanne Highley, my spiritual mother, and Ron Highley, who truly has been like a father to me. I am glad to have had the honor of being your "unnatural" daughter.

Damsel Plum and Mirah Riben, for excellent proof-reading and editing, wonderful review comments, and giving of their valuable time and expertise.

To the King of Kings, who has opened the doors that no man can shut, and shut the doors that no man can open.

The Lord giveth and the Lord taketh away: blessed be the name of the Lord.

If you would like more information about searches or ALMA please contact:

The ALMA SOCIETY
P.O. Box 727 Radio City Station
New York, NY 10101-0727
212. 581.1568
almainfo@aol.com
www.almanet.com

About The Author

Vida Theresa Rodriguez Farrisi was born and raised in Manhattan and received her education at Sarah Lawrence College, Mannes College of Music, and Skidmore College, through which she received her degree in music. Theresa's first book *Diaper Changes: The Complete Diapering Book and Resource Guide* has been received to critical acclaim and was a 1998 Writer's Digest National Self-Published Book Award winner.

Theresa's first recording, *Lullabies: Traditional American and International Songs* has been released and she is currently working on her third book *Babywise Is Not Wise*.

Besides singing and writing, Theresa enjoys her avocation as a seamstress and being a "keeper at home." She created her company so that she could enjoy the presence with her young children that a home-based business affords.

Theresa would someday like to produce an historical church hymnal, a recording of early American hymns and songs, a recording of the songs of Stephen Foster, and a modern edition of the poetry of George Herbert.

Theresa's husband Tony designs and creates their line of hardwood blocks sets called ECOBLOCKS. Together they are parents of six homeschooled children: Francesca, Angelica, Anthony, Gloria, Gabriella and Sophia.

The Farrisi's make their present home in Pennsylvania Dutch Country.

Diaper Changes: The Complete Diapering Book and Resource Guide

by Theresa Rodriguez Farrisi

The Diapering Bible!

If you have diapering questions, *Diaper Change*s has the answers! Loved by moms everywhere!
Recommended by Dr. Bill and Martha Sears, Mothering Magazine and La Leche League International!

1998 WRITER'S DIGEST NATIONAL
SELF-PUBLISHED BOOK AWARD WINNER !!!!!

Cloth Diapers? Diaper covers? Diaper services? Disposables? Confused by the many diapering choices? Looking for a special cloth diapering product? Don't want to waste a lot of time on the internet? Would you like mother-to-mother support? Could you use to save some money and energy? You have just discovered the ONLY BOOK available on diapering in America today! **Diaper Changes: The Complete Diapering Book And Resource Guide** is everything today's parents need to know about diapering options, issues, and resources.

* Theresa tried every cloth diaper, cover and accessory out there— so you don't have to!
* why waste time searching through dead links, weird diapering sites, or web clutter?
* over 60 mail-order sources in one place: no other way to find it all easily
* fully Revised 2nd Edition has websites, email, new companies, products and more!
* Find anything from organic cotton diapers to Gore-Tex covers to wool soakers
* hard-to-find adult and youth incontinence products
* no ad hype: just scores of honest product reviews from experienced mother of five!
* find your own balance between cloth and disposables; know your potential health and safety risks
* diaper patterns and fabric sources for the creative or frugal soul
* know all your options and avoid buying inferior cloth diapering products!
* loads of illustrations, practical info, and encouragement

"I am very impressed with Diaper Changes... I think it will become the "Diapering Bible," much like The Womanly Art of Breastfeeding has become the "Breastfeeding Bible". —North Carolina

"Absolutely fantastic!" —Texas

"Kudos! Bravo! God bless you! Your thorough research, beautiful writing style and masterful editing made your book not just an excellent "resource guide" as your subtitle indicates, but also sheer joy to read. I had no idea I'd enjoy reading a book about diapering so much. I carried it everywhere I went from the bath tub to my bed for nursing sessions, to every minute I could catch, until I had finished. Your love and devotion to your God-given role as mother is evident on every page. And the familiar style with which you approached the writing made me feel as if I was reading a long letter from an old friend. Again, I thank and applaud you." —New Jersey

"The info in Diaper Changes was lifesaving." — Massachusetts

"I have really enjoyed Diaper Changes—I've recommended it to 3 friends already. It opened up a whole new world of diapering styles and products to me— what a great help! Thank you!" — Pennsylvania

"I really love Diaper Changes! It's laid some great groundwork for those of us just starting out with babies. Your book really made me feel confident about homewashing my own diapers. Thanks again for this great resource!" — California

"Thank you for writing Diaper Changes... I wish I had found it before my son was born— I could have saved a lot of money!" — Connecticut

"Diaper Changes is great! I'm 38, 6 months pregnant for the first time, and didn't know where to start regarding cloth diapering.... I hadn't realized the vast amount of choices we had! Thanks for making it easier to make up our minds." —Texas

"Diaper Changes was fun to read, very informative and honest, too. A wonderful book." — Minnesota

"Awesome" —California

"I loved Diaper Changes..wonderful for new moms to get connected to the parenting world."– Minnesota

"Since I received Diaper Changes I haven't been able to leave it alone! I've been laughing, nodding my head in agreement the whole time like a bobby-headed dashboard dog and yes, sometimes crying as I read. Everything is right on the button." — Colorado

"Diaper Changes is great! I enjoyed the upbeat, chatty style of writing and the extremely helpful information." — North Carolina

"Thanks so much for a wonderful, insightful book! You've really helped me make my diapering experience enjoyable and fun!" — Massachusetts

"I feel like I know you so well after reading Diaper Changes... thank you for writing such a great book. I will spread the word!" — California

"Thank you so much for writing such a wonderful book packed with information— I feel proud of my decision to switch from disposables to wonderful cotton. Again, thank you for your marvelous work in Diaper Changes." — California

To order please use the order form enclosed with this book or call 877.285.4337
or visit the DIAPER CHANGES website at www.diaperchanges.com

𝔏𝔲𝔩𝔩𝔞𝔟𝔦𝔢𝔰
𝔗𝔯𝔞𝔡𝔦𝔱𝔦𝔬𝔫𝔞𝔩 𝔄𝔪𝔢𝔯𝔦𝔠𝔞𝔫 𝔞𝔫𝔡 𝔍𝔫𝔱𝔢𝔯𝔫𝔞𝔱𝔦𝔬𝔫𝔞𝔩 𝔖𝔬𝔫𝔤𝔰
𝔗𝔥𝔢𝔯𝔢𝔰𝔞 ℜ𝔬𝔡𝔯𝔦𝔤𝔲𝔢𝔷 𝔍𝔞𝔯𝔯𝔦𝔰𝔦

Voice, guitar, autoharp, Appalachian mountain dulcimer

"This incredible vocalist must be experienced to be believed... a rare and gifted performer who specializes in early American and Anglo-American folk songs . . . mesmerizing." — **Acoustic Cafe Review**

"LULLABIES is deeply haunting in a lovely way, meditative, spiritual, operatic, folksy, nurturing, cozy.... tender treatment of classics lulling me calm... a little chunk of heaven." — Colorado

"In the insert with LULLABIES you say that "these pieces are among the most beautiful and haunting melodies in existence." I've got to tell you that they would not be so "beautiful and haunting" if somebody else were singing them. Your voice is so incredible. My toddler came over and sat on the floor next to me when the tape started. After a few minutes he crawled into my lap and decided that this music was nursing music. It's quite a compliment when you can grab the attention of a toddler and hold it. Thanks!" —Utah

"LULLABIES is soothing, lyrical, really beautiful! There is nothing else like this music currently available. It is one of my daughter's favorite recordings!"—Massachusetts

❖❖❖❖❖❖❖❖❖❖❖

SIDE ONE:
Hush A Bye, Don't You Cry
Twinkle, Twinkle/Rock A Bye Baby/Bye Baby Bunting (medley)
Nani, Nani
Durme
Christ Child's Lullaby
Hush, My Babe, Lie Still In Slumber
Angels Watching Over Me
All Through The Night

SIDE TWO:
Hush Little Baby, Don't Say A Word
Rozhenkes Mit Mandlen
Oif'n Pripechuck
Bye'M Bye
Coventry Carol
Resonet in Laudibus
Venid Pastorcicos
Brahm's Lullaby (Lullaby and Good Night)

❖❖❖❖❖❖❖❖❖❖❖

To order please use the order form enclosed with this book or call 877.285.4337
or visit our website at www.homekeepers.com/lullabies.html

ECOBLOCKS™: Handcrafted, Heirloom-Quality, Natural Oil-Finished, 100% Reclaimed Hardwood Blocks At Excellent Prices!

WHY ECOBLOCKS™?

• ECOBLOCKS are lovingly handcrafted from reclaimed, untreated hardwoods— saving precious trees and landfill space. No trees are harvested directly to make these block sets.

• ECOBLOCKS are finished with a specially prepared, non-toxic, natural linseed oil treatment— no icky shellac or varnish here! Safe enough for even your youngest teething baby to get a hold of!

• ECOBLOCKS come in a beautiful, unique assortment of sizes and shapes, textures and hues— knots, grain variations, shadings and all— for hours of wholesome, creative play.

• ECOBLOCKS offer you more blocks for the money! Unlike other block sets which are expensive and really don't give enough blocks to "do anything", we have decided from the onset to provide enough blocks in our Ecoblocks sets to have plenty to play with.

• ECOBLOCKS sets are carefully crafted by hand, with tools commonly found in a professional woodworking shop. Many hours are spent designing and creating each ECOBLOCKS set.

• ECOBLOCKS come packaged in a heavyweight, durable, recyclable plastic storage container for lots of daily use.

"Your ECOBLOCKS are really lovely! My kids played with them for hours and hours! Extremely well made, beautifully finished, perfectly sized, and so, so reasonable!   —Colorado

In your ECOBLOCKS set you will get:
* 4 or more different hardwoods
(maple, oak, cherry, mahogany, walnut, poplar, aspen, cedar, others as available)
* 8 different sizes of blocks
* 4 basic shapes
(rectangles, squares, logs, triangles)
* a beautiful, unique combination of shades, hues and textures—
no two sets exactly alike!!!
150 UNIQUE, HANDCRAFTED PIECES
FOR ONLY $99.95!
50 per cent more than other comparable sets!!
HALF SETS ALSO NOW AVAILABLE-
75 PIECES ONLY $49.95!!

For ECOBLOCKS 150-piece set:)
* 30 small rectangles (2 1/4" x 1 1/2" x 1/2")
* 30 medium rectangles (4 3/4" x 3/4" x 1/2")
* 10 large rectangles (6" x 2 1/2" x 7/8")
* 20 small logs (2 3/4" x 3/4" x 3/4")
* 20 large squares (3" square x 3/4")
* 20 small squares (2 1/4" square x 3/4")
* 10 small triangles (3" base)
* 10 large triangles (4 1/4" base)

For ECOBLOCKS 75-piece set:
* 15 small rectangles (2 1/4" x 1 1/2" x 1/2")
* 10 medium rectangles (4 3/4" x 3/4" x 1/2")
* 10 large rectangles (6" x 2 1/2" x 7/8")
* 10 small logs (2 3/4" x 3/4" x 3/4")
* 10 large squares (3" square x 3/4")
* 10 small squares (2 1/4" square x 3/4")
* 5 small triangles (3" base)
* 5 large triangles (4 1/4" base)

PLEASE NOTE: We can even make a custom set to match your specifications of woods, shapes, or sizes, usually at no extra charge!!! Just call! We GUARANTEE your satisfaction!!

WE HAVE MUCH MORE TO SHOW YOU ABOUT ECOBLOCKS. EVERY SIZE BLOCK, QUANTITIES, COLORS OF WOODS, AND MORE! OR VISIT OUR WEBSITE AT **www.ecoblocks.com** TO VIEW OUR ONLINE, FULL-COLOR BROCHURE ANYTIME!

How To Order:
Your ECOBLOCKS set will be custom-crafted just for your family. It will take 4-6 weeks to complete your order and will be shipped via Parcel Post or RPS. Shipping charges are $10.00 for the 75-piece Half Set and $18.00 for the 150-piece Full Set in the US only. California, Oregon and Washington State please add $5.00 shipping surcharge. We are not shipping Ecoblocks to Canada or overseas at this time. Your satisfaction is absolutely guaranteed. Returns are accepted within 30 days of the date your order is shipped. All shipping and return shipping charges are non-refundable. We accept Visa and Mastercard and your card will not be billed until your order is shipped. You may order via our website, our toll-free number, or by sending a check or money order with the enclosed Homekeepers order form on the facing page. Shipping rates subject to change. All block sizes are approximate and are subject to variation based on availability of woods.

Homekeepers Publishing
P.O. Box 439
Richland, PA 17087
877.285.4337
fax 717.866.2661
orders@homekeepers.com
www.homekeepers.com

ORDER FORM

You may use this order form, or if you prefer, you may call our toll-free number, send a fax, or use our secure online order form. For wholesale inquiries please contact the publisher.

Visit our website for more info and updates on all of our products!
www.homekeepers.com
Coming soon: Homekeepers Journal!

WHEN
ADOPTION
FAILS
$11.95 each

DIAPER
CHANGES
$14.95 each

Item wanted	How many?	Total

	Shipping	
	6% sales tax (PA residents only)	
	Total of order	

LULLABIES
$14.95 cassette
$15.95 CD

ECOBLOCKS
$289.95 150-piece Full Set plus 10.00 s/h
$144.95 75-piece Half Set plus $18.00 s/h
California, Oregon, and Washington State please add extra $5.00 shipping surcharge

Shipping charges: $3.00 Priority Mail up to any 4 items, (except ECOBLOCKS). Canadian orders: please add additional $6.00 to total (U.S. funds only)
Foreign orders: please add $9.00 to total (U.S. funds only)

I am paying by: ____Check   ____ M.O.   ____VISA   ____MC

Send to:_____   Bill to: _____

_____   _____

_____   _____

Card#: _____   Phone#: _____

Signature:_____   Exp date: _____

All sales final. Please allow up to 2 weeks for delivery. Thanks for your order!